Questions of Evide

The Twentieth Century World

Peter Mantin

To my parents

Hutchinson Education

An imprint of Century Hutchinson Ltd
62–65 Chandos Place, London WC2N 4NW

Century Hutchinson Australia Pty Ltd
PO Box 496, 16–22 Church Street, Hawthorn,
Victoria 3122, Australia

Century Hutchinson New Zealand Limited
PO Box 40-086, Glenfield, Auckland 10
New Zealand

Century Hutchinson South Africa (Pty) Ltd
PO Box 337, Bergvlei 2012, South Africa

First published 1987

Reprinted 1987

© Peter Mantin

Set by Rowland Phototypesetting Ltd
Bury St Edmunds, Suffolk

Printed and bound in Great Britain

British Library Cataloguing in Publication Data
Mantin, Peter
    Questions of evidence: the twentieth
    century world.
    1. Great Britain – History – 20th century
    I. Title
    941.082   DA566
    ISBN 0 09 170221 6

Contents

Working with evidence

Finding out about the past

There are two ways in which we can find out about the past:
(1) We can read books or watch TV programmes made by people who have studied the past.
(2) We can look at what people who were there at the time in the past wrote, photographed, drew or painted and then make up our minds.

The ways in which we find out about the past are called sources of evidence. Any of these sources may tell us different things about the past, so we need to know what we can learn and what we should beware of whenever we look at sources of evidence.

Have a look at this example of a famous event in British history, the general strike of 1926 and see if you can come up with your own idea of what probably happened. Since this strike took place over 60 years ago there is a problem of 'distance'. Most of us weren't even born when the general strike took place, so we have to rely on what other people said and thought about it – and many of those people are now dead. People disagree about almost everything, so it isn't surprising that this one event should be seen differently, or that people should 'take sides'.

Different points of view can be detected in the four pieces of evidence shown below. Besides looking at what they said, see if you can work out how you might decide why they might be different from each other, and what each of the sources of evidence might tell us about what actually happened.

Before you look at the sources, it is useful to know that the general strike was called by the Trades Union Congress on May 3 1926. It collapsed nine days later. Unlike an ordinary strike, a general strike invites all trades union workers to stop work. It was called in support of the miners, who wanted better working conditions, and involved millions of workers, not only in rail, transport and communications, but in many other industries. The government strongly opposed the strike and did everything it could to make sure that work in the country did not come to a standstill. During the strike, politicians, trades union workers and newspaper owners tried very hard to produce news-sheets and newspapers, so as to let the public know what was happening. Here are four of those pieces of news:

A From *The British Gazette*, May 6 1926 (the official government newspaper).
"The general strike is a direct challenge to ordered government. It is an attempt to force on some 42,000,000 British citizens the will of less than 4,000,000 others, working in the vital services of the country.

The strike is intended as a direct hold-up of the nation to ransom. It is for the nation to stand firm in its determination not to give in. 'This moment', as the Prime Minister pointed out in the House of Commons, 'has been chosen to challenge the existing Constitution* of the country and to substitute the rule of force for that which now exists . . . I do not believe the workers were consulted before this terrible power was put into the hands of a small committee in London . . . I do not think all the leaders who agreed to order a general strike fully realised that they were coming nearer to proclaiming civil war than we have been for centuries past.' "
Note – 'constitution' means the way in which the country is run.

B From *The British Worker*, May 7 1926 (the official strike news bulletin published by The General Council of the Trades Union Congress).
"The General Council does not challenge the constitution. It is not seeking to substitute unconstitutional government. Nor is it trying to weaken parliament. The only aim of the Council is to get for the miners a decent standard of life. The Council is engaged in an industrial dispute.

It is . . . fantastic for the prime minister to pretend that the trade unions are engaged in an attack upon the constitution of the country. The General Council is determined to maintain the struggle strictly on the basis of an industrial dispute. They have ordered every member taking part to behave perfectly and not to give any cause for police interference. The General Council struggled hard for peace. They want an honourable peace as soon as possible. They are not fighting the community. They are defending the mine workers against the mine-owners.''

1 On what points do these two accounts differ? Use extracts from the accounts to support your answer.

2 Why do you think these two accounts are so different?

3 What other evidence might help you check these stories?

C From *The Daily Herald*, May 4 1926.
"The miners have been locked out of the pits, so as to force them to accept lower wages and longer hours. The government stands behind the mine-owners. It has rejected the trade union movement's every effort to bring about an honourable peace.

The talks that had begun on Saturday were ended suddenly in the early hours of yesterday morning by the government. Despite this, the whole labour movement, including the miners' leaders, continued its efforts yesterday. But unless a last minute change of heart by the government takes place during the night, the country will today be forced, by the action of the government, into an industrial struggle bigger than this country has yet seen.

The prime minister showed no sign of going back on his opinion that negotiations could not begin whilst the general strike order stood, and unless lower wages were accepted before talks began. The central fact stands out that the blame for the crisis rests with the government and the mine-owners.''

D From *The Times*, May 6 1926
"Since a general strike has been ordered, the nation is called on to support the government which was placed in power by a huge majority of the votes of the people. The duty to obey this call is clear. The nation will not allow the trades unions to take over from parliament, or to ignore the wishes of the people. No government worthy of the name can give up the duty with which the people trusted it. The people would never forgive the breaking of such a promise.

The people have followed with warm admiration the never ending efforts of their government to bring about a peaceful settlement of the problem and to avoid the ruin of a general strike. The nation has approved of trade unionism when trade unionism has been conducted in a reasonable way. But a general strike causes terrible damage on the community as a whole. They are committing a dangerous crime against the nation and will be punished for it.''

4 Does *The Daily Herald* (Document C) agree more with Document B or with Document A? Support your answer by quoting from Document C.
5 Which 'side' do you think *The Times* (Document D) was on during the general stike? Explain your answer.
6 Why is it hard to find out who was to blame for the general strike? Give reasons for your answer.

Asking questions

It may not be easy to make sense of what happened in the past, but it need not be impossible! Indeed, once we have the sources of evidence, four key operations help us to decide why they might be different from each other, and what each might be able to tell us about what actually happened. These questions are:
● Who wrote or made the evidence? What is his or her point of view? What does he or she know about the subject?
● When was it written or made? Was the person there at the time? How much longer after the event was it written down or made?
● What is it? Is it an eye-witness account, a newspaper report, a private letter, a photograph, a poster, a cartoon, a painting?

● Why was it written or made? Did the author have a particular purpose which might have affected how it was done?

Who wrote or made the evidence?

When we looked at the general strike we saw very different descriptions of what the strike was about from different people involved at the time. All of these people could be writing something they really believed to be true. But in telling their story they would have wanted to remain loyal to their 'side'. Perhaps they might even have been tempted to alter or exaggerate the facts. You would have to take this into account in deciding what to believe. This is true of other historical evidence. Have a look at the two newspaper reports below. They are describing the same event, the Battle of the Somme (Britain and France against Germany) during the first world war, yet they give very different impressions of what happened.

A Extract from a British newspaper, *The Daily Mirror*, July 3 1916.

B Extract from a German newspaper, *Frankfürter Zeitung*, July 3 1916.

Translated from the *Frankfürter Zeitung*.

ANGLO–FRENCH OFFENSIVE
ENEMY'S HEAVY LOSSES AND NEGLIGIBLE GAINS
15 Enemy Planes Shot Down
......
Advance on Eastern Front
......

General Headquarters, 2 July
Correspondent: W. B. Amtlich

Western Theatre of War

After a whole week of the most heavy artillery and gas bombardment, there began today on a broad front of about forty kilometres the great Anglo–French massed offensive, which has been under preparation—with limitless resources—for many months.

On both banks of the Somme, from the river Ancre at Gommecourt to the La Boisselle area the enemy gained no advantage worth mentioning, but suffered heavy losses. Nevertheless, on both French and British Somme fronts their assault troops managed to penetrate our front line in isolated spots. It was preferred therefore to withdraw our divisions from the front-line trenches, which had been completely destroyed by heavy fire, to the reserve line between the first and second positions.

As is usual in such circumstances, some material—permanent fixtures of the front line—having been rendered useless, was lost.

1 Who is the enemy in Document A?
2 Who is the enemy in Document B?
3 On what points do the two accounts differ? Use extracts from the accounts to support your answer.
4 Why do you think the stories are so different?
5 Make a list of the events of the Battle of the Somme which you think did actually happen from Documents Ⓐ and Ⓑ.
6 What other evidence might help to decide what happened?

The reason for the differences has something to do with the fact that they are looking at the same thing from differerent points of view. We use the word bias to describe the telling of a story from one point of view. Sometimes the bias is very obvious – as in the two newspapers shown here. On other occasions we might not be so sure. There is no such thing as a totally unbiased description, because everybody tells a story from his or her own point of view. Just because two stories are different, it doesn't necessarily mean that either of them is 'lying' or is useless to the historian. To reconstruct the past, historians look at a number of different sources and try to check or 'confirm' what one source says, by looking at another source.

When was it written?

One way of deciding the importance of different sources is to find out how close they were to the event they describe. Historians divide these sources into two groups – primary and secondary sources.

A 'primary source' is a piece of evidence that came about at the time of the event it describes – in other words, it is the original material. A 'secondary source' came into being later – it is often based on the original.

Sort out the following list of sources about the Battle of the Somme, 1916, into two headings – primary sources and secondary sources:
● Photographs of soldiers at the battle.
● Letters home from soldiers at the front.
● History book 'The Somme' written in 1967.
● Map of troop movements drawn by a general during the battle.
● School history book, mentioning the battle, published in 1973.
● Machine-guns and grenades found on the battlefield.

● Computer simulation game 'The Somme'.
● Newspaper editorial written in London 1916.

Most of these should fit easily into one of the two groups. A primary source might tell us more clearly what it was like to be there at the time. A secondary source might give us some clearer background or put an event into a wider picture, to help us understand it. So primary sources are not necessarily better nor more accurate than secondary sources.

Look at this secondary source, a book called 'The General Strike' by R. J. Cootes, published in 1964:

"The first day of the strike had given rise to a number of wild rumours, especially in outlying districts of the country. Some people said that it was a revolution, and that strikers and police were fighting pitched battles in the streets. It was feared that there would be no food left after a few days, and, in some places, it was believed that the government and the Royal Family had all fled to France! All of these stories were, of course, quite untrue, but it was difficult to deny them while the strike of newspaper printers continued.

People thirsted for news. When it became known that some of the smaller papers printed outside London had not yet ceased publication, there was a great rush for copies.

Both the government and the TUC realized the great power of the press. If they wanted to gain public support for their respective viewpoints, they would have to produce newspapers. Printers had to be found somehow, Winston Churchill had some experience of journalism, and he soon gathered round him a band of loyal supporters at the Argus Press, the home of the *Morning Post* (a paper which is no longer produced today). A newspaper, representing the interests of the government, was produced with the aid of 'blackleg' printers for the first time on May 5. It was called *The British Gazette*.

The TUC was not to be outdone. Arrangements were quickly made to take over *The Daily Herald* offices and produce a paper called *The British Worker* to put the trade union side of the question. On the evening of May 5, the first edition was ready. Both papers sold at one penny each. While *The British Gazette* was trying to persuade people that the strike was a failure and would soon collapse, *The British Worker* was keen to give the impression that everything was going according to plan. As you know from the facts mentioned in the previous chapters, neither of these reports was absolutely correct!"

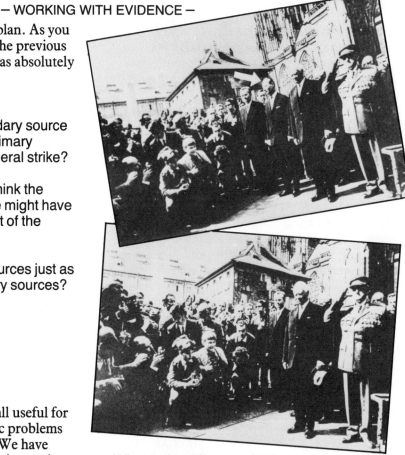

Q

1 What do we learn in this secondary source that helps us understand the primary newspaper accounts of the general strike?

2 What primary sources do you think the author of this secondary source might have used, so as to write this account of the general strike?

3 In what ways are secondary sources just as useful to the historian as primary sources?

What is the difference? What seems to have happened? Suggest reasons why.

What is it?

The sources we have looked at are all useful for historians, but there may be specific problems associated with particular sources. We have already seen that newspaper reports in wartime may be biased according to 'the side they are on', so we need to examine them critically.

By looking carefully at different sources of evidence and discovering what they are, we may learn more about how useful and reliable they are in finding out about the past.

Photographs

Since the beginning of photography in the nineteenth century, photographs have been a helpful way of looking at things we cannot see for ourselves. After all, everybody knows that 'the camera never lies' – or does it?!

Have a look at the two photographs (top right) of a meeting of Czech communist leaders in Prague. The arrow points to an important difference in the pictures, which claim to be of the same event. Even if photographs are not altered deliberately to be misleading, they will still not necessarily tell us the whole truth.

The 'doctored' photograph has removed the Czech Communist leader Alexander Dubcek, who went out of favour with the Russians, which led to the Russian invasion of Czechoslovakia in 1968.

A 'Official' photograph of Hitler.

The fact that the photograph was 'doctored' might tell us a lot about the people who doctored it!

Q What do you think it tells us about them?

Photographs may make events 'credible' in a way that words don't. However, we shouldn't assume that a lot of the photographs we deal with are 'doctored'. Most photographs show us things that do exist, but we cannot guarantee that they tell us everything. Photographs can give us very different impressions of the same event or person, according to who is holding the camera and what is seen in the picture. So we need to treat a photograph just like any other source of evidence and decide how reliable it is by asking

Who made it?

Why was it made?

Look at the two photographs of Adolf Hitler. They are both helpful to us in learning about Hitler, but in different ways.

B Elderly Hitler with a young girl.

Q

1 What do you think we learn about Hitler from looking at Document **A**? (Carefully describe Hitler, his clothes, the expression on his face etc.)

2 What do you think we learn about Hitler from Document **B**? What is the difference between the two photographs? How has our impression of Hitler changed?

3 Document **A** was taken for a reason – to make a point. Explain why you think the photograph was taken, and what Hitler wanted people who saw the photograph to think of him.

4 Why might Hitler not have wanted to have Document **B** published?

So, like any other source of evidence, photographs have their strengths and weaknesses.

5 In what ways might a photograph be a useful source of evidence for historians?

6 In what ways might a photograph not be a very useful source of evidence for historians?

Paintings

Sometimes historians have no photographs to use, so they may turn to other 'visual' sources such as paintings. However, when doing so, the historian has to be aware of the same difficulties and ask him or herself the same questions as when dealing with photographs – or indeed with any other source of evidence. Paintings may also be biased.

Biographies

Read this secondary source. It is an extract about a painting of Hitler by Klaus Richter. This extract is taken from a biography or lifestory by Robert Waite, titled 'The Psychopathic God, Adolf Hitler', 1977.

"The circumstances in which this portrait was painted were remarkable. Richter had been invited in 1941 to do a portrait of Reich Marshal Hermann Göring. When he learned that a visit from Hitler was expected, it was arranged for him to sketch the Führer, with the proviso that he do so from a well-concealed hiding place. Richter was unimpressed with Hitler's face until someone mentioned the word 'Jew'. When Hitler heard that word, Richter later recalled, his face was immediately transformed into something at once demonic and defensive, a haunting look which Richter quickly sketched and, later that night, put down in oils. He labelled it 'A German Worker' and hung it in a shed where it survived the war. Richter had also painted Field Marshal von Schlieffen, Chancellor Stresemann and President of the Reichstag Löbe, but he considered the Hitler portrait to be his masterpieece. The art critic of *Die Zeit* called it 'the only really authentic portrait of Hitler . . . perhaps the most important historical portrait that any German artist has ever had the opportunity to paint'."

Q 1 What do we learn about Hitler from this biography? Support your answer by quoting words from the biography.

2 How do you think the biography might have been different, if it had been written by a supporter of Hitler?

3 Make a list of primary sources that a biographer of Hitler might use.

Film
One of the primary sources that the biographer of Hitler might use is film. Look at these frames from a film taken by Walter Frenz in 1940, showing Hitler hearing the news of the surrender of the French forces.

1 Why might a film of Hitler be thought to be even more useful than some other primary sources to the historian of Hitler as evidence?

However, the historian has to be careful when using any source of evidence – even film. For example these frames of the film were 'looped' (repeated) together by a Canadian who was an enemy of Hitler's, to give a misleading idea of what was happening in the film.

2 What do you think the Canadian who 'looped' the film together wanted people who saw the film to think about Hitler?

Of course, we would not expect most films to have been tampered with, or 'doctored'. Yet, like all other sources, film makes more sense as evidence if the historian asks questions about it – particularly who made the film and why.

Hitler hears the news of the surrender of the French forces

Why was it written?
The author of a piece of writing, cartoon, etc. may have particular reasons for doing what he did.

It is part of the historian's job to detect these reasons and understand what attitudes and ideas are being put across. This of course is very useful as it reveals a great deal about the attitudes and ideas of people or groups at a particular time in history.

Propaganda
Look at the pictures from a children's book (opposite page). We may think of asking why things are included in children's books, but in this case that question is particularly important.

These pictures are taken from the Nazi children's book 'Trust No Fox and No Jew'. On the left can be seen the 'true German' and on the right is the 'Jew' (picture A).

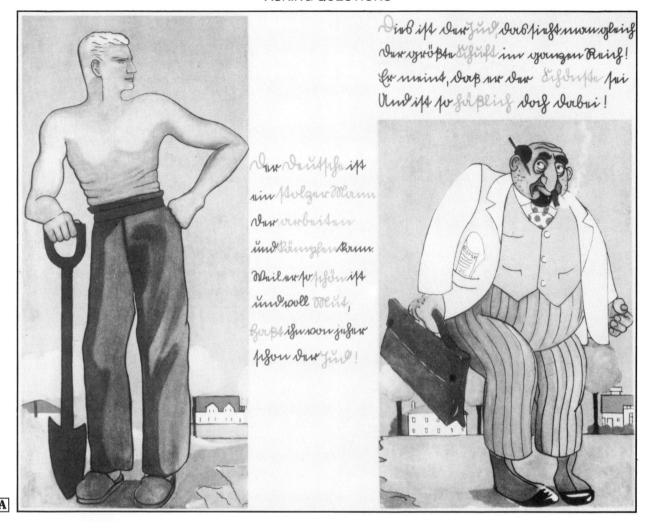

Q1 Describe what you see in pictures A. What were the children supposed to think when they saw these pictures?

Picture B was taken from the same book. The Jewish teacher and children are being expelled from the school so that 'discipline and order' can be taught properly.

Q2 Describe what you see in picture B and explain what children who saw the picture were supposed to think about Jews.

Historical documents may be understood differently at different times. Children who see this picture today and who knew what happened to the Jews in the second world war might understand this picture differently from the children who first saw it in Nazi Germany.

Q3 How might children studying history today understand this cartoon (picture B)?

The Nazi children's pictures you have seen could be called 'propaganda', because they set out to appeal to the emotions and feelings of the readers to put across a particular set of views and ideas.

This deliberate bias can be seen in some of the evidence that is set out in this book. Recognising propaganda is an important and useful skill, and it is vital to bear in mind the question 'why is the source written or made' since propaganda involves such a deliberate intention on the part of the person who made or wrote the source of evidence that you probably need to look at the other side of the story to get a full picture.

Posters
Look at this British second world war poster, showing Winston Churchill, the British prime minister.

Q1 Describe what it shows and explain why you think it was produced.

Q2 What do you think the person who drew the poster wanted someone who saw it to think?

Cartoons
Now look at the political cartoon below. These cartoons aren't always meant to be funny. They are drawn for a reason. The cartoonist is trying to make a point or put across an idea or an opinion.

Your understanding of this cartoon may be helped if you know something of the background to the times in which it was drawn.

BARBARISM   CIVILIZATION

A British cartoon by David Low, October 12 1935.

In the autumn of 1935, Benito Mussolini, the
leader of Italy, ordered his troops to attack the
north-east African country of Abyssinia (now
called Ethiopia). Mussolini wanted to build an
Italian empire in Africa and was prepared to
ignore the criticism of many other countries –
that he had no right to launch this invasion. The
Abyssinians, armed only with primitive weapons,
were crushed by the Italian armed forces, which
used tanks, aeroplanes and gas to gain victory.

[Q] What does the cartoon show and why do you
think it was drawn? What point do you think the
cartoonist was trying to make?

Writing a good answer

In this book you will have to try and work out
what different pieces of evidence mean. Don't
worry if it's not always easy – you may be facing
similar problems to those encountered by
professional historians. Try to bear in mind the
simple questions to ask about a source that we've
met in the introductory section.

Think of *when* the source was written or made,
whether the source is *primary* or *secondary*, and
how it may have been understood at the time it
was written or made. Ask yourself *what* it is and
what its usefulness to the historian is likely to be.
Above all, to understand what the evidence
means, remember the last of those questions,
namely *why* was it written or made? Back up your
ideas or hunches by quoting or copying evidence
from the sources. Your answers will therefore
stand a much better chance of being impressive,
because you'll have given reasons for what you
write.

1.1   **Trench war**

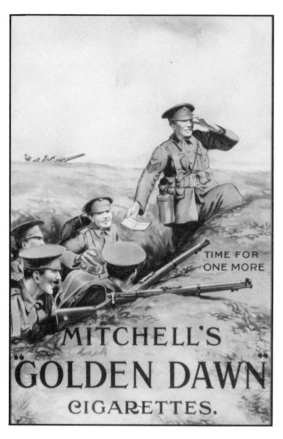

A Poster, 1915.

B **Extract from 'Victorian Son: An Autobiography, 1897–1922' by Stuart Cloete.**
"Burial was impossible. In ordinary warfare the bodies went down with the limbers that brought up the rations. But then there were seldom more than three or four in a day. Now there were hundreds, thousands, not merely ours but Germans as well. And where we fought several times over the same ground bodies became incorporated in the material of the trenches themselves. In one place we had to dig through corpses of Frenchmen who had been killed and buried in 1915. These bodies were putrid, of the consistency of Camembert cheese. I once fell and put my hand right through the belly of a man. It was days before I got the smell out of my nails. I remember wondering if I could get blood poisoning and thinking it would be ironic to have survived so much and then be killed by a long-dead Frenchman."

C **From 'Eye-Deep In Hell', by John Ellis, published in 1979.**
"One British private said that his 'overriding memory of all his time on the western front was the smell'. Another in his diary, spoke of 'a penetrating and filthy stench . . . a combination of mildew, rotting vegetation and the stink which rises from the decomposing bodies of men and animals. This smell seems a permanent feature of the firing line.' The odour was almost unbearable in the great charnel houses of the front, Ypres, the Somme, Verdun. When the Germans captured Côte 304 at Verdun in May 1916 one of the first demands of the conquering troops was for a double ration of tobacco to mask the overwhelming stink of the corpses. A Frenchman who fought in this sector wrote 'We all had on us the stench of dead bodies. The bread we ate, the stagnant water we drank, everything we touched had a rotten smell, owing to the fact that the earth around us was literally stuffed with corpses'."

Document questions

1 According to Document [A], what was life like in the trenches for the soldiers? Support your answer by describing the poster.

2 According to Document [C], why did the soldiers want cigarettes? How is this different from the idea given in the poster?

3 Why do you think it was so difficult to bury the bodies of the soldiers? (Document [B])

4 Look at Documents [B] and [C]. Write sentences to explain two things on which Documents [B] and [C] agree. Each of the two explanations has to be supported by quotations, one from Document [B] and one from Document [C].

5 Look again at Documents [B] and [C]. Which one is the primary source and which one is the secondary source? Explain your answer.

6 Why do you think Document [A] is so different from the two other documents? Give reasons for your answer and remember to include what the document is and why it was produced.

Follow-on questions

7 Write a letter home from the trenches. The letter is from a soldier who has seen Document [A] and then goes to the trenches and discovers what conditions are really like.

1.2   **A new kind of war**

A **Extract from a cavalry training manual, 1907.**
"It must be accepted as a principle that the rifle, effective as it is, cannot replace the effect produced by the speed of the horse, the magnetism of the charge, and the terror of cold steel."

B **Statement by Joffre, 1912.**
"The French army, returning to its traditions no longer knows any other law than that of the attack. All attacks are to be pushed to the limit, with firm determination to charge the enemy with the bayonet, in order to destroy him."

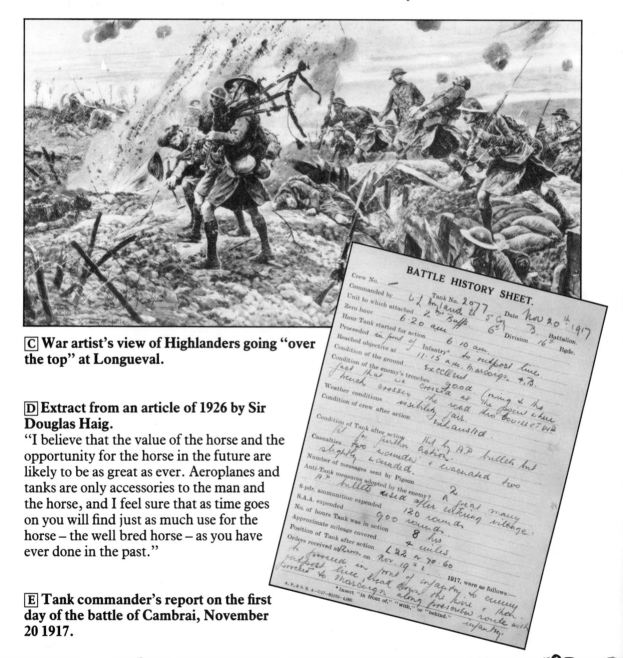

C **War artist's view of Highlanders going "over the top" at Longueval.**

D **Extract from an article of 1926 by Sir Douglas Haig.**
"I believe that the value of the horse and the opportunity for the horse in the future are likely to be as great as ever. Aeroplanes and tanks are only accessories to the man and the horse, and I feel sure that as time goes on you will find just as much use for the horse – the well bred horse – as you have ever done in the past."

E **Tank commander's report on the first day of the battle of Cambrai, November 20 1917.**

Document questions

1 *Read Document* A.
 a Write a couple of sentences to explain in your own words what the author of Document A expected the war would be like – you don't have to quote the actual words of the document.
 b Why do you think the author of Document A thought that the war would be like this?

2 *Read Document* B. Did Joffre expect a similar or a different kind of war from that described in Document A? Explain your answer.

3 **a** *Look at Document* C. It shows what the war was really like.
 Write sentences to describe three things in the photograph and explain how they show that this was 'a new kind of war'.
 b What doubts would the historian of the first world war have about using photographs (as in Document C) as evidence?

4 Why do you think Document D was written and what does it tell us about Haig's views on warfare?

5 *Read Document* E. Using the evidence in Document E, write a paragraph to describe what we learn about how tanks were used in battle in this 'new kind of war' and what conditions were like for the tank crews.

Follow-on questions

7 Who was Joffre? (See Document B.)

8 How do the views of Haig and Joffre in Documents B and D help explain the slaughter of trench warfare?

9 Did Haig's predictions about what war would be like in the future turn out to be correct or incorrect? Explain your answer.

10 Why did it become necessary to use tanks in the first world war? What was it hoped that tanks would achieve?

1.3 Women at war

A **Postcard issued by the National Union of Women's Suffrage Societies.**

B **Poster authorised by Lord Baden-Powell, 1915.**

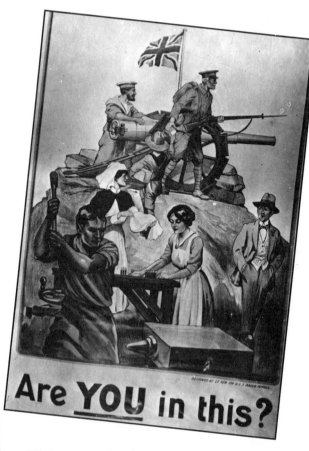

C **Extract from 'Suffragettes International' by Trevor Lloyd, 1971.**
"People admired the women who went off to work in shell factories, pouring liquid TNT into the canisters, running the risk of being blown up or – less drastic but still unpleasant – being stained bright yellow by picric acid. No doubt some of the munitions workers were making a sacrifice for the war effort; however many of them had been doing more uncomfortable jobs for equally long hours at lower wages and with much less security of employment in the years before the war.

Women who had never previously worked did not often go into factory jobs. But many more nurses were needed than before, and many of the new recruits were women from the comfortable classes who felt that they were now doing something useful; it was an unfortunate side-effect that their willingness to work for low wages encouraged everybody to think nursing was a vocation for which a living wage was quite unnecessary."

D The proportion of female to male employment in the UK, 1914–20.

(Figures are percentages)

	Industry	Transport	Government establish-ments	Agricul-ture	Commerce and finance	Local govern-ment	Total of all employment
July 1914	26	2	3	9	27	34	24
July 1918	35	12	47	14	53	52	37
July 1920	27	4	5	10	40	36	28

Document questions

1 *Look at Document* A. Who do you think were the 'National Union of Women's Suffrage Societies' and what clue is shown in the postcard as to what they wanted?

2 *Look at Document* B.
   a Name two jobs done by women in wartime.
   b What do you think was the aim, or purpose, of the poster? Explain your answer and support it by mentioning points from the poster.

3 *Read Document* C.
   a Suggest two reasons why women who had not worked before the war chose nursing, rather than factory, work.
   b What clue is there in the document which might help explain why women eventually got the vote after the first world war?

4 *Look at Document* D.
   a What was happening to the numbers of women in employment between 1914 and 1918? Support your answer with figures from the table and suggest a reason for your answer.
   b What was happening to the numbers of women in employment between 1918 and 1920? Support your answer with figures from the table and suggest a reason for your answer.

Follow-on questions

5 Is Document C a primary source or a secondary source? Explain your answer.

6 What organization did Lord Baden-Powell (author of Document B) set up?

1.4   **War posters**

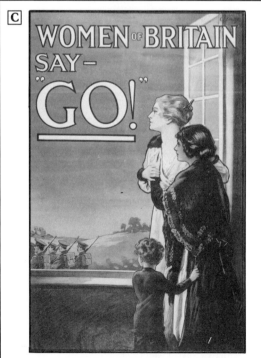

Document questions

1 a Name the country which the 'mad brute' in Document A stands for. Mention one clue from the poster to back up your answer.
   b What do you think the aims of Document A were? What were the men who saw the poster supposed to think and do? Mention clues from all the posters.

2 a What do you think the aims of Document B were? Give reasons for your answer.
   b In what important ways do you think Document B is similar to Document A? Explain your answer.

3 What, according to Document C, should women's contribution to the war be?

4 Document D is one of the most famous of all war posters. Describe what it shows and explain what you think made it so special.

5 These posters could be described as 'propaganda' because they deliberately put across ideas and views that only tell one side of the story. Give examples from Documents B and D to show how they are propaganda.

Follow-on questions

6 Why, especially in the first two years of the war, was it particularly important for the government to issue posters like these?

7 Which of the four posters do you think was probably *not* a British poster? Give a reason for your answer.

8 You are an artist, working for the British government; sketch a design for a poster. It must:
   a have a patriotic message,
   b encourage people to join the army, and
   c encourage people to hate the enemy.
Make sure your poster does all three of these things, but doesn't just copy any other poster. It should be a first world war poster, not a later one.

1.5   Versailles

"PERHAPS IT WOULD GEE-UP BETTER IF WE LET IT TOUCH EARTH"

A British cartoon, 1921.

B **Extract from the Treaty of Versailles, 1919.**
"*Article 231*   The allied governments affirm and Germany accepts the responsibility of Germany and her allies for causing all the loss and damage to which the allied governments and their nationals have been subjected as a consequence of the war imposed upon them by the aggression of Germany and her allies."

C **Speech by Georges Clemenceau, 1918.**
"We shall seek only peace, which we intend to make just, solid, so that those who come after us may be spared the abominations of the past."

D **Extract from 'Ten Years After', by Sir Philip Gibbs, 1929.**
"It was a peace of vengeance. It reeked with injustice. It was on the economic side of the treaty and in its interpretation that the statesmen of the allies seemed to be stricken with insanity. Germany, they insisted, had to pay all the costs of the war, for the damage she had inflicted and the ruin she had caused. But, justice or injustice apart, the wild impossibility of extracting all that vast tribute from the defeated enemy ought to have been manifest to the most ignorant schoolboy."

Document questions

1 *Look at Document* A.
   a What is the 'indemnity' shown weighing down the cart?
   b Which countries did Briand and Lloyd George come from?

2 *Read Document* B.
   a Why was Germany so angry about this part of the treaty? Support your answer with a quotation from Document B.
   b Is Document B a primary or a secondary source? Give a reason for your answer.

3 What do you think Clemenceau was talking about in Document C when he mentioned 'the abominations of the past'?

4 *Read Document* D *and look at Document* A. Do you think Sir Philip Gibbs' opinion about the Treaty of Versailles was similar or different from that shown by the person who drew Document A? Mention things seen in the cartoon in your answer.

Follow-on questions

5 By what other name was Article 231 known? (Document B)

6 Who was Clemenceau? (Document C)

7 Find examples from the Treaty to show how Clemenceau (Document C) made sure that his own country would be 'solid' and well-protected?

2.1 America and the League

A Extract from 'Britain and the World since 1970', by H. K. Middleton.
"Congress refused to agree to the peace treaty, and kept the USA out of the League. Many American politicians claimed that the USA had already won the war for the allies. Now Europe and the rest of the world should try to solve their own problems. In the meantime, the allied countries should pay back to the USA all the money they had borrowed to fight the war."

ANOTHER "RESERVATION."
Starving Europe. "GOD HELP ME!"
America. "VERY SAD CASE. BUT I'M AFRAID SHE AIN'T TRYING."

B British cartoon, 1920.

C Speech by Woodrow Wilson, 1919.
"The question is whether we can refuse the moral leadership that is offered us, whether we shall accept or reject the confidence of the world."

D Speech by Theodore Roosevelt, 1919.
"Mr Wilson has no authority whatsoever to speak for the American people at this time . . . His fourteen points and his four supplementary points and all his utterances every which way have ceased to have any shadow of right to be accepted as expressive of the will of the American people."

E From 'The Forgotten Men of Versailles', by Harry Hansen.
"The great achievement of the peace conference was the League of Nations. Even though the American Congress rejected the work of an American president, it is a milestone in the history of man's slow progress towards the control and outlawry of war. For twenty years afterwards the American people deluded themselves that, because the League sat in far-off Geneva and we had no official association with it, it did not concern us. Without our political support, the League was preponderantly a British bulwark, and it could not make its sanctions against Italy effective in the Ethiopian crisis. It took a second world war, with its terrible cost, to bring the United States into the United Nations. If a nation can sit in sackcloth and ashes, the United States should do so for its selfish rejection of the League."

Document questions

1 *Read Document* [A].
   a What is 'Congress'?
   b Give two reasons why Congress rejected the Treaty and the League (either give quotations from Document [A] or write it in your own words).

2 *Look at Document* [B].
   a What points do you think the person who drew the cartoon was trying to make?
   b Mention points from the cartoon and back up your explanation by quoting a sentence from Document [A] which makes a similar point.

3 Who was Woodrow Wilson, and how do you think he might have replied to Theodore Roosevelt's accusation in Document [D] that 'Mr Wilson has no authority whatsoever to speak for the American people'?

4 To which 'peace conference' is the author of Document [E] referring?

5 Would the author of Document [E] have agreed more with the ideas of Woodrow Wilson (Document [C]) or Theodore Roosevelt (Document [D])? Write a couple of sentences to explain your answer and support it with a quotation from one of the documents.

Follow-on questions

6 Which one of Theodore Roosevelt's relatives later became famous in American history? Explain why he became famous.

7 What was it about the League of Nations which made it 'a milestone in the history of man's slow progress towards the control and outlawry of war' (Document [E])? Explain in your own words why the League was so important.

8 **a** *Read Document* [E]. How did America's attitude towards the League help lead to its failure in the Ethiopian crisis? Explain your answer and support it with a quotation from the document.
   b *Read Document* [D]. What was the idea behind the 'fourteen points' referred to in Document [D]? Write a few sentences to explain what these 'fourteen points' had to do with the 'moral leadership' Wilson talks about in Document [C]. You don't need to quote from the documents.

2.2 President F. D. Roosevelt

A Photograph of Roosevelt's birthplace and family home, Hyde Park, New York.

B Photograph of President Roosevelt pitching the opening ball of the 1941 baseball season at a Washington stadium.

C Description of Roosevelt's recovery from an attack of polio in 1921 taken from 'Franklin Roosevelt', a biography by Hugh Talbot, 1950.

"In a letter of 1924 Franklin wrote: 'This condition of extreme discomfort lasted about three weeks. I was then moved to a New York hospital, and finally moved home in November, being able by that time to sit up in a wheel-chair, but the leg muscles remained extremely sensitive and this sensitiveness disappeared gradually over a period of six months. . . .'

The above is, of course, an understatement. It says nothing of the weary weeks in bed with heavy plaster casts on his legs to stretch the muscles. It says nothing of the torture caused each day by the chipping away of a bit of the plaster from the back of his legs to add to the pull of the muscles. It says nothing of the agony of mind of a strong, athletic, ambitious man in the prime of life who is suddenly made almost helpless, and who sees himself laid aside on the shelf – temporarily, at any rate – just when he has really begun to make his mark.

It looked as though he would be condemned to the life of a more or less helpless invalid.

The same spirit of iron strength and dogged perseverance that triumphed over physical disability, showed itself in the man who led his country into action against economic disaster and inspired the world in its battle for freedom."

D **Table of American presidential election figures, 1940–1944.**

ROOSEVELT'S FIRST ELECTION ───────────

Place of Nominating Convention	Chicago
Ballot on Which Nominated	4th
Republican Opponent	Herbert Hoover
Electoral Vote	472 (Roosevelt) to 59 (Hoover)
Popular Vote	22,815,785 (Roosevelt) to 15,759,266 (Hoover
Age at Inauguration	51

ROOSEVELT'S THIRD ELECTION ───────────

Place of Nominating Convention	Chicago
Ballot on Which Nominated	1st
Republican Opponent	Wendell L. Willkie
Electoral Vote	449 (Roosevelt) to 82 (Willkie)
Popular Vote	27,243,466 (Roosevelt) to 22,304,755 (Willkie)
Age at Inauguration	58

ROOSEVELT'S SECOND ELECTION ───────────

Place of Nominating Convention	Philadelphia
Ballot on Which Nominated	1st
Republican Opponent	Alfred M. Landon
Electoral Vote	523 (Roosevelt) to 8 (Landon)
Popular Vote	24,751,597 (Roosevelt) to 16,697,583 (Landon)
Age at Inauguration	54

ROOSEVELT'S FOURTH ELECTION ───────────

Place of Nominating Convention	Chicago
Ballot on Which Nominated	1st
Republican Opponent	Thomas E. Dewey
Electoral Vote	432 (Roosevelt) to 99 (C vey)
Popular Vote	25,602 5 (Roosevelt) to 22,00 ?7ʒ (Dewey)
Age at Inauguration	62

Document questions

1 What does Document **A** show and why might it be useful to a historian writing a biography of Roosevelt as evidence? Explain your answer.

2 **a** According to Document **D**, how successful a politician was Roosevelt? Quote figures from the table to support your answer.
  b What difference do you notice in the way American presidents are elected from the way in which British prime ministers are chosen from the evidence of Document **D**?

3 What does the photograph in Document **B** show and what political reasons can you suggest to explain why President Roosevelt might want people to see this photograph?

4 **a** What source of evidence has the author of Document **C** quoted to support his description of Roosevelt's recovery from polio?
  b The attack of polio took place over 11 years before Roosevelt became President, so why do you think the author of Document **C** has thought it important to include this information in a biography of Roosevelt? Support your answer with a quotation from Document **C**.

Follow-on questions

5 **a** Name two other sources *not* already mentioned in these documents that might be useful to a historian writing a biography about Roosevelt as evidence. Explain your answer carefully.
  b What evidence is there that the author of Document **C** was biased in favour of Roosevelt?
  c If Document **C** is biased, does that mean it is useless to the historian of Roosevelt?

2.3   Marshall plan

A **From a speech by American Secretary of State George C. Marshall, June 15 1947, at Harvard.**

"The world situation is very serious: the physical loss of life, the destruction of cities, factories, mines and railroads, the dislocation of the entire fabric of the European economy. The breakdown of the business structure of Europe during the war was complete. Europe's requirements for the next three or four years of foreign food are so much greater than her present ability to pay that she must have substantial additional help or face very serious economic, social or political problems.

It is logical that the United States should do whatever it is able to do to assist in the return of normal economic health in the world. Our policy is directed not against any country or doctrine but against hunger, poverty, desperation and chaos. Any government that is willing to assist in the task of recovery will find full cooperation. Any government which tries to block the recovery of other countries cannot expect help from us. Governments, political parties or groups which seek to perpetuate human misery in order to profit therefrom politically or otherwise will encounter the opposition of the United States.

The role of this country should consist of friendly aid in the drafting of a European program. The program should be a joint one, agreed to by a number, if not all, of the European nations."

B **British cartoon, 2 March 1948.**

"WHO'S NEXT TO BE LIBERATED FROM FREEDOM, COMRADE?"

C **From a speech at the United Nations, September 18 1947, by Andrei Vyshinsky, Soviet Deputy Minister for Foreign Affairs.**

"The Marshall plan is merely a variant of the Truman doctrine. It is becoming more and more evident to everyone that the implementation of the Marshall plan will mean placing European countries under the economic and political control of the United States and direct interference by the latter in the internal affairs of those countries.

Moreover this plan is an attempt to split Europe into two camps and, with the help of the United Kingdom and France, to complete the formation of a bloc of several European countries hostile to the interests of the democratic countries."

D **Soviet cartoon (with translated captions) from magazine, 1948.**

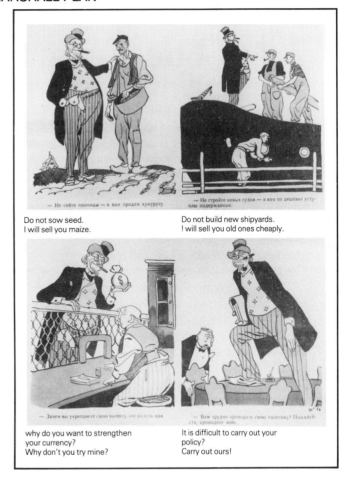

Do not sow seed.
I will sell you maize.

Do not build new shipyards.
I will sell you old ones cheaply.

why do you want to strengthen your currency?
Why don't you try mine?

It is difficult to carry out your policy?
Carry out ours!

Document questions

1 Give two reasons, according to Document **A**, to explain why Europe needed the Marshall plan.

2 Do you think the person who drew Document **B** approved or disapproved of the policies of the man shown on the left hand side of the cartoon? Explain your answer and support it by mentioning two things from the cartoon.

3 Would the author of Document **C** have agreed or disagreed with the claim made in Document **A**, that the Marshall plan was 'directed not against any country or doctrine, but against hunger, poverty, desperation and chaos'? Write a sentence to explain your answer and support it with a quotation from Document **C**.

Follow-on questions

4 **a** According to Document **D**, what is 'Uncle Sam' trying to do and how does he go about doing it?
  b Does Document **C** give a similar, or different, view of what 'Uncle Sam' wanted from that suggested in Document **D**? Explain your answer.
  c How can we define 'propaganda'?

2.4 The Truman doctrine

A Part of a speech given by President Truman to Congress, March 12 1947.
"At the present moment nearly every nation must choose between alternative ways of life.

One way of life is based on the will of the majority and is distinguished by free institutions, representative government, free election, guarantees of individual liberty, freedom of speech and election and freedom from political oppression.

The second way of life is based upon the will of a minority forcibly imposed on the majority. It relies upon terror and oppression, a controlled press and radio, fixed elections and the suppression of personal freedoms.

I believe that it must be the policy of the United States to support free peoples who are resisting attempted subjugation by armed minorities or by outside pressures. I believe that our help should be through economic and financial aid. In helping free and independent nations to maintain their freedom, the United States will be giving effect to the principles of the Charter of the United Nations.

It is necessary only to glance at a map to realize that the survival and integrity of the Greek nation are of importance in a much wider situation. If Greece should fall under the control of an armed minority the effect upon its neighbor Turkey would be immediate and serious. Confusion and disorder might well spread throughout the Middle East.

The free peoples of the world look to us for support in maintaining their freedoms."

B American cartoon, 1947.

C Speech at the United Nations, 18 September 1947, by Andrei Vyshinsky, Soviet Deputy Minister for Foreign Affairs.
"The so-called Truman doctrine is a particularly glaring example of the way in which the principles of the United Nations are violated, of the way in which the United Nations is ignored. The United States has moved towards giving up the idea of international cooperation and joint action by the great powers. It has tried to force its will on other independent countries, whilst at the same time obviously using the money distributed as relief to needy countries as an instrument of political pressure.

This is clearly proved by the measures taken by the United States government with regard to Greece and Turkey, which ignore and bypass the United Nations. This policy conflicts sharply with the principle expressed by the General Assembly in its resolution of 11 December 1946 which declares that relief supplies to other countries should, at no time, be used as a political weapon."

D Soviet cartoon, 1948.
The caption reads 'Defenders of Greece. Forward, Your Country Needs You'.

«ЗАЩИТНИКИ» ГРЕЦИИ

Рис. Л. БРОДАТЫ

— Вперёд! Этого требует наСША родина!..

Document questions

1 Which two countries' ways of life were being described by Truman in paragraphs 2 and 3 of Document A? Give the names of the countries and quote the words which describe their way of life.

2 a Name the man shown in Document B.
 b Do you think the person who drew Document B was a supporter or an opponent of the Truman Program? Support your explanation with a description of the cartoon and a quotation from Document A.

3 Was America following the principles of the United Nations in the Truman doctrine? Compare what Documents A and C say. Write 'yes' or 'no', explain your answer and back it up with a quotation.

4 a *Look at Document* D. Which country does the man on the left, holding the gun, come from?
 b Do you think the person who drew Document D was a supporter or an opponent of the Truman Program? Support your explanations with a description of the cartoon and a quotation from Document C.

5 Documents B and D could both be called 'biased' sources of evidence. Does that mean they're useless to the historian of the Truman doctrine? Explain your answer.

Follow-on questions

6 What is 'Congress'? (Document A)
7 Why did Truman introduce his 'doctrine'? In a paragraph describe the events which had led Truman to believe he had to do something positive.
8 What had happened in the second world war to leave America in a much better position than the Soviet Union to provide 'money distributed as a relief to needy countries'?

2.5   The Korean war

A **From 'The Roots of European Security' by Vadim Nekrasov, published in 1984.**
"But disarmament was the opposite of American plans of political and economic expansion in Europe, Asia and other parts of the world, forming new military-political alliances. Hence its opposition to all peace proposals.

The American military intervention in Korea in the summer of 1950 aggravated the already tense international relations. The United States, having landed troops in Southern Korea after Japan's surrender in 1945, was seeking to gain control of the whole country.

By unleashing a civil war in June 1950 the South Koreans, backed by the United States, turned the Korean peninsula into an arena of fierce international conflict but in the end failed to achieve the aims of its Washington masters. Soviet and Chinese assistance to the People's Democratic Republic of Korea frustrated the plan to take over North Korea."

B **Soviet cartoon, 1950.**

Korea

Iran   Turkey   Taiwan

C **Statement by United States President Truman, June 27 1950.**
"In Korea the government forces were attacked by invading forces from North Korea. The UN security council called on the invading troops to cease hostilities and to withdraw to the 38th parallel. This they have not done, but on the contrary they have pressed the attack. The security council called on all members of the United Nations to give assistance. I have ordered US air and sea forces to give the Korean government troops cover and support.

The attack upon Korea makes it plain beyond all doubt that communism has passed beyond the use of subversion to conquer independent nations and will now use armed invasion and war. It has defied the orders of the security council, issued to preserve international peace and security. A return to the rule of force in international affairs would have far reaching effects. The United States will continue to uphold the rule of law."

D British cartoon, 1950.

Document questions

1 **a** Write a sentence to explain what the Americans' world-wide plans were. Support your explanation by quoting a sentence from Document A and by describing what you see in Document B.

   b According to Document C, what were the ambitions, or plans, of Soviet communism? What similarity do you notice between this and the Soviet view, in Document A, of America's plans?

2 Compare the Soviet version of how the Korean War started (Document A), with the American version (Document C). What important difference do you notice? Quote from both documents to support your answer.

3 Why do you think Truman is so keen to mention the United Nations (Document C)?

4 **a** What doubts would the historian of the Korean War have in accepting Soviet history books (as in Document A) as evidence?

   b Choose *three* of the things shown in Document D and explain carefully how *each* of them backs up the American side of the Korean War story (Document C).

Follow-on questions

5 What was the '38th parallel' (Document C)?

6 What do you think Truman was referring to in Document C when he warned of a 'return to the rule of force in international affairs'?

7 Name the man shown in the poster at the top right of Document D.

8 If the two stories of how the Korean War began are so different, must that mean that one of them is lying? Explain your answer.

2.6 Vietnam – guerilla war

A **From Tom O'Brien's 'If I Die in a Combat Zone', 1973.**
"Along the way we encountered the citizens of Pinkville; they were children under ten years, women, old folks who planted their eyes in the dirt and were silent. Where are the VC? (Viet Cong). No answers, not from the villagers. Another futile search. The men were becoming angry and there were no enemy soldiers to shoot back at, only hedgerows and bushes. In the next days it took little provocation for us to flick the flint of our Zippo lighters. Thatched roofs take the flame quickly and on bad days the hamlets of Pinkville burned, taking our revenge in fire. It was good, just as pure hate is good.

We walked to other villages and the phantom 48 Viet Cong Battalion walked with us. When a booby-trapped artillery round blew two popular soldiers into a hedgerow, men put their fists into the faces of the nearest Vietnamese, two frightened women, and when the troops were through with them, they hacked off chunks of thick black hair.

Jet fighters were called in. The hamlet was leveled and napalm was used. I heard screams in the burning black rubble."

B **From an article by freelance reporter Martha Gellhorn published in *The Guardian*, September 1966.**
"To really and truly and finally win this war we must . . . win the hearts and minds of the people of South Vietnam . . . however . . . we, unintentionally are killing and wounding three or four times more people than the Vietcong do, so we are told, on purpose. We are not maniacs and monsters, but our planes range the sky all day and all night, and our artillery is lavish and we have much more deadly stuff to kill with. The people are there on the ground, sometimes destroyed by accident, some destroyed because Vietcong are reported to be among them. This is indeed a new kind of war, as the indoctrination lecture stated, and we had better find a new way to fight it. Hearts and minds, after all, live in bodies."

C **South Vietnamese children fleeing from a napalm attack.**

Document questions

1 How does Document [A] help us understand why American soldiers destroyed Vietnamese villages with 'little provocation' and treated Vietnamese civilians so badly?

2 Quote two phrases or sentences from Document [A] which give us clues about the fighting methods of the Vietcong. In each case write another sentence to explain why you think they used these methods.

3 What reasons can you find in Documents [A] and [B] to explain why so many American soldiers became so disillusioned or fed up with the type of war they faced in Vietnam?

4 What are the advantages and disadvantages, to the historian of Vietnam, of the memories of an American soldier (as in Document [A])?

5 In the light of what you have read in Documents [A] and [B], why do you think Document [C] made such an impact on the millions of people who saw it? Explain your answer.

Follow-on questions

6 Write a couple of sentences to explain what you think the author of Document [B] meant when she wrote 'Hearts and minds, after all, live in bodies'.

7 Draw a poster – either in favour of American involvement in the war, or against the American presence in Vietnam. You get marks for including things which give reasons and explain the idea behind the poster.

2.7 Lenin, Stalin and Trotsky

A Statement by Stalin, 1924.
"As for Trotsky, he was a coward during the time of the Brest Litovsk negotiations and the greatest victories during the Civil War were won in spite of him. Neither in the party, nor in the uprising did Trotsky play any special role, nor could he do so for in the October Days he was relatively new in our party."

B Painting by the Soviet artist Kibrik, painted after Lenin's death, titled 'Comrades-in-arms at the First All-Russian Congress of Soviets, June 1917'

C From 'The Rise and Fall of Stalin' by R. Payne, 1965.
"Stalin, by introducing the cult of the dead Lenin, was reinforcing his own role as Lenin's successor. He was the faithful 'comrade-in-arms', the man who always stood beside Lenin at moments of danger or at moments of great decision. There began to appear drawings and paintings which showed them in discussion. They had rarely been photographed together. Soon the existing photographs would be doctored to show them sitting very close to one another."

D From Lenin's Political Testament, 1923.
"Comrade Stalin, having become general secretary, has concentrated enormous power in his hands; and I am not sure that he has always known how to use that power with sufficient caution. Stalin is too rude and this fault becomes insupportable in the office of a general secretary. Therefore I propose to the comrades to find a way to remove Stalin from the position and appoint to it another man who in all respects differs from Stalin in one superiority – namely, that he is more patient, more loyal, more polite and more considerate to comrades, less capricious etc."

Document questions

1 **a** Name two complaints made by Stalin about Trotsky in Document A.
 b How do you think a supporter of Trotsky might have replied to *each* of these criticisms?

2 *Look at Documents* B *and* C. Who probably ordered Document B to be painted and why? Say what the painting shows and quote from Document C to support your answer.

3 **a** *Read Document* D. What do you think a 'political testament' is?
 b What does it tell us about Lenin's attitude towards Stalin just before he died?

4 **a** *Compare Documents* B *and* D. In what ways does the evidence from Document D give us a different picture of the relationship between Lenin and Stalin?
 b Suggest a reason for this difference.
 c Which source do you think gives a more accurate picture of the relationship between Lenin and Stalin – Document B or Document D? Explain why.

5 Using the evidence in the documents write a paragraph to explain what we learn about Stalin's character. Support your answer with two quotations.

Follow-on questions

6 What happened at 'Brest Litovsk' and in the 'October days' (Document A)?

7 Why do you think Lenin ordered his 'political testament' to be written? What do you think he was trying to achieve in it?

8 Which of the documents might most accurately be described as 'propaganda'? Explain your answer.

9 *Look at the documents about the 'show trials' (page 42).* How justified was Lenin's warning in his testament, that Stalin had not 'always known how to use power with sufficient caution'? Support your answer with two quotations.

2.8 Collectivisation

A Soviet cartoon about collectivisation.

B Parts of speeches by Stalin in January 1933 and February 1934.

"The task of the five year plan was to transfer our country with its backward technology on the lines of modern technology. The task was to convert the USSR from an agrarian and weak country, dependent on the whims of the capitalist countries, into an industrial and powerful country. The party was so confident in the plan that it decided to undertake the task, not in five years but in four. We did not have an iron and steel industry, now we have one. We did not have an industry for producing modern agricultural machinery, now we have one."

C From Victor Serge's 'Memoirs of a Revolutionary, 1901–1941', published in 1963.

"The winter was frightful despite the lessening of the famine towards the New Year. I went to hospital in Orenburg. It was run as efficiently as possible but really all that it treated was poverty. It was filled with those whose sickness lay in undernourishment. Children were covered in cold sores; whole wards were full of peasants with bellies empty, worn-out clothes. Medical supplies were in such short supply that the same bandages were washed out and used over and over again. Nor shall I forget in those miserable days how we all heard a radio broadcast from a meeting of the workers of a collective farm. Passionate voices went on endlessly thanking the 'leader' for the 'good life we lead' and twenty or so patients tortured by hunger, half of them collective farm workers themselves listened to it all in silence."

D Table of Soviet grain harvests and procurements (in millions of tonnes).

	1928	1929	1930	1931	1932	1933
Grain harvest	73.7	71.7	83.5	69.5	69.6	68.4
State grain procurements	10.8	16.1	22.1	22.8	18.5	22.6
Livestock (million head)						
Cattle	70.5	67.1	52.5	47.9	40.7	38.4
Pigs	26.0	20.4	13.6	14.4	11.6	12.1
Sheep and goats	146.7	147.0	108.8	77.7	52.1	50.2
*Tractors	0.0	—	—	—	—	1300.0

* *No figures available for 1929–1932.*

Document questions

1 *Look at Document* A.
   a Tell the story shown in the pictures of the cartoon.
   b Why do you think the cartoon was produced? What was the purpose behind it?

2 *Compare Documents* B *and* D and explain whether the figures in the table tend to agree or disagree with the following statement made by Stalin in Document B: 'We did not have an industry for producing modern agricultural machinery, now we have one'. Write 'agree' or 'disagree', explain your answer and support it with figures from Document D.

3 What other types of figures, not included in Document D, would be useful in checking the other claims made by Stalin in Document B? Explain your answer.

4 a *Compare Documents* B *and* C. Would the author of Document C have been impressed or not with Stalin's speech in Document B? Explain your answer and support it by mentioning two things Serge saw in Document C.
   b Do the figures in Document D back up Serge's views in Document C of what conditions were like in the USSR? Give an example.
   c Suggest a reason why Document B may be called a biased source of evidence about life in the USSR in the early 1930s.

Follow-on questions

5 Who were the Kulaks and why were they so opposed to collectivisation?

6 Suggest reasons:
   a why Stalin introduced collectivisation, and
   b why it proved so difficult to put into practice.

7 What were the costs to the Russian people of the enforced introduction of collectivisation?

2.9   **The show trials**

A **From 'Stalin: A Political Biography' by I. Deutscher, 1949.**

"Among the men in the dock were all the members of Lenin's politbureau except Stalin himself and Trotsky, who, although absent, was the chief defendant. All were charged with working from the earliest days of the revolution for the spy services of Britain, France, Japan and with plotting with the Nazis to destroy the Soviet Union. All loudly confessed their sins. Their confessions were the only basis for the verdicts. A hotel where three of the accused were said to have met Trotsky had actually closed down years before their 'meeting'. The defendants hoped that their confessions would save their families; and they may also have had a glimmer of hope to save themselves. Stalin's real motive was to destroy the men capable of forming an alternative government."

B **From R. Hingley's 'Joseph Stalin: Man and Legend', 1974.**

"The Zinoviev trial was an act of murder performed by Stalin. From the start the rigging of the trial was closely planned by Stalin in person. He had many ways of making his victims talk. Held in isolation for months or even years on end, deprived of sleep, beaten night and day, the defendants were usually more than half broken already when confronted with the signed confessions of associates previously brainwashed. Stalin would shout that Zinoviev and Kamenev were to be 'given the works' until they came crawling on their bellies with confessions in their teeth. Zinoviev was influenced by threats to his family, being also subjected to the physical ordeal of a cell deliberately overheated in the height of summer, which was additionally troublesome in view of his poor health. The dictator did, however, give his personal word that neither Zinoviev nor Kamenev would be executed if they would stand trial on his terms. It was on the basis of this lying assurance that the two chief victims finally went to their doom. Once the trial had been successfully concluded Stalin ordered Yagoda to execute 5,000 former opponents already under arrest."

C **Cartoon from the Soviet magazine 'Krokodil', 1936**

Trotsky

Kamenev   Zinoviev

Document questions

1 The trials described in these documents were known as 'show trials'.
   a What do you think a 'show trial' is? Explain your answer carefully and back it up with a quotation from Document [A] or Document [B].
   b Write a sentence to explain why you think Stalin held these trials, and back it up with a quotation from Document [A].

2 Suggest two reasons why people admitted to 'crimes' they had not committed.

3 a Who and what does Document [C] show?
   b How do you think Document [C] is connected with the changes described in Document [A]? Support your explanation with a quotation from Document [A].

4 Using the evidence from the documents write a paragraph to explain what you think we learn about Stalin's character. Support your ideas with quotations from the documents.

Follow-on questions

5 *Look at Document [A].*
   a Why do you think Trotsky was the chief defendant?
   b What fate did Trotsky suffer in Mexico in 1940?

6 Who were Zinoviev and Kamenev (Document [B])?

2.10 The birth of NATO

A From 'NATO – an Information Leaflet' published by the British Atlantic Committee, 1984.

"NATO is an alliance of Western nations, equal in status, formed in 1949 with twelve members. It was formed to counter the aggressive behaviour of the Soviet Union which, having taken over parts of Finland and the Baltic States during the second world war, continued such actions in Eastern European countries in 1945. By the end of 1947, the rest of Romania, Poland, Bulgaria and Hungary were also behind the iron curtain, to be followed in 1948 by Czechoslovakia after a coup d'état. That same year saw the beginning of the siege of West Berlin which lasted until May 1949. It is a defensive military alliance."

B From 'The Roots of European Security' by Vadim Nekrasov, 1984.

"Churchill's speech in Fulton on March 5 1946, attacked the Yalta and Potsdam agreements. In the presence of President Truman, Churchill called on the US and British governments to take a hard line towards the USSR, threatened to use the American A-bomb and insisted on forming a military alliance against the USSR. But the Soviet Union did not give up its hopes that co-operation would continue.

The founding in April 1949 of NATO was clearly aimed at preparing for war against the USSR. For example, the chairman of the appropriations committee said that Washington would use NATO to obtain air bases in Europe, from where air strikes could be made on Moscow. Thus Washington's foreign policy was still based on the US monopoly of the A-bomb. After that the Soviet Union made it clear that NATO's members had broken with the ideas of the anti-Nazi coalition in the war years."

C Soviet cartoon 1949, entitled 'Solemn Signing of the Atlantic Pact'.

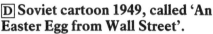

D Soviet cartoon 1949, called 'An Easter Egg from Wall Street'.

The innocent dove is painted on the egg. But we, dear reader, shall have a look at what is under the shell, inside the egg.

The lid is off. Look! Uncle Sam was hiding inside with his secret. He threatens with his bomb anybody who will not be his slave.

Here is the second secret of the Easter egg. Behind Uncle Sam hides Winston Churchill the highwayman.

And finally – look what's hidden. Hitler is making a deal with Wall Street.

Document questions

1 a Name the country which, according to Document **A**, was responsible for the 'aggressive behaviour' that led to the forming of NATO.
b Quote two examples from Document **A** of that country's 'aggressive behaviour'.

2 *Compare Documents **A** and **B***. What difference do you notice in the way they show what type of alliance NATO is and what its aims are? Explain your answer and support it with quotations from both documents.

3 *Look at Document **C***. Do you think the person who drew the cartoon would agree with the statement in Document **A** that: 'NATO is an alliance of Western nations, equal in status'? Support your explanation by mentioning things in the cartoon.

4 Write sentences to explain what you think the person who drew Document **D** was trying to say about NATO by including each of these things:
a 'The innocent dove' (part 1),
b Uncle Sam with his 'A' Bomb (part 2), and
c Winston Churchill the highwayman (part 3).
Include quotations from Document **B** if you think they help to explain your answer.

Follow-on questions

5 a What were the most important of the 'Yalta and Potsdam decisions' (Document **B**)?
b *Read Document **B***. List the accusations made against Churchill. Then read the documents about the 'Iron Curtain' (page 52). What differences do you notice between these accusations and what Churchill actually said?

2.11 Czechoslovakia 1968

[A] Announcement from the Presidium of the Czechoslovak Communist Party Central Committee, broadcast on Prague radio, August 21 1968.

"To the entire people of the Czechoslovak Socialist Republic. Yesterday on 20 August around 11 p.m. troops of the Soviet Union, Polish People's Republic, East Germany, the Hungarian People's Republic and the Bulgarian People's Republic crossed the frontiers of the Czechoslovak Socialist Republic.

This happened without the knowledge of the president of the Republic, the chairman of the national assembly, the premier or the first secretary of the Czechoslovak communist party central committee.

In the evening hours the presidium of the Czechoslovak communist party central committee had discussed preparations for the 14th Czechoslovak communist party congress.

The Czechoslovak communist party central committee presidium appeals to all citizens of our republic to maintain calm and not to offer resistance to the troops on the march. Our army, security corps and people's militia have not received the command to defend the country.

The Czechoslovak communist party central committee presidium regards this act as against not only the fundamental principles of relations between socialist states but also as against the principles of international law."

[B] Soviet statement issued by the press agency, Tass, August 21 1968.

"Party and government leaders of the Czechoslovak Socialist Republic have asked the Soviet Union and other allied states to give brotherly help with armed forces. This request was brought about by the threat from counter-revolutionary forces. The troops will be withdrawn as soon as the threat to Czechoslovakia and neighbouring communist countries has been eliminated.

The actions that are being taken do not attack the interests of any country. They serve the purpose of peace. The brotherly countries are firmly resisting any threat from outside. Nobody will ever be allowed to break a single link from the chain of Socialist countries."

[C] Czechoslovakian street cartoon, 1968.

D Photograph taken in Prague, Czechoslovakia, 1968.

Document questions

1 *Read Document* A. Why do you think the Czechoslovakian communist party central committee:
   a didn't order its army to 'defend the country', but
   b wanted to show that the Soviet intervention in Czechoslovakia was 'against the principles of international law'?
   Each time give one reason, but explain it carefully.

2 *Compare Documents* A *and* B. Name two ways in which they disagree about what was happening in Czechoslovakia. Each time write a sentence to explain your answer and support it with quotations from both documents.

3 Explain carefully why you think these two versions (Documents A and B) of what was happening were so different.

4 Do you think Document A is a primary source or a secondary source? Explain your answer.

Follow-on questions

5 *Look at Document* C.
   a Who is the man in the cartoon? What point do you think the cartoonist is trying to make?
   b Which version of what was happening in Czechoslovakia – Document A or Document B – does the photograph (Document D) seem to support or agree with more? Give reasons for your answer.
   c What doubts might the historian of Czechoslovakia 1968 have in using press statements as evidence?

2.12 Solidarity

A **Extract from the demands of the striking shipyard workers at the Lenin Shipyard, Gdansk, August 14 1980.**

a) Official trade unions should be disbanded in favour of freely elected, independent unions.

b) The 'commercial shops' should be closed and meat prices be restored to their former subsidised levels.

c) A general wage rise of 2,000 zlotys (about £30) per month should be paid in Gdansk.

d) Pensions and family allowances should be increased.

e) Three sacked shipyard workers should be reinstated.

f) A monument should be set up to remember workers killed in the 1970 riots.

g) These demands should be published by the mass media.

B **Extract from an interview given on Polish television by Mr Edward Babiuch, Prime Minister of Poland, August 15 1980.**

"I sharply criticise these interruptions of work and warn workers to return to their employment. The public is not sufficiently aware of the severe financial pressures on the Polish economy; food price rises will not be withdrawn. Poland's enemies are exploiting the situation to the country's disadvantage. The situation is worrying Poland's friends but our allies believe that we shall be able to resolve our difficulties on our own."

C **Cartoon in the *Sunday Times*, August 24 1980.**

D **Extract from a 21-point agreement between the government commission and the inter-factory committee in Gdansk, August 31 1980.**

"The activities of the trade unions in Poland have not fulfilled the hopes and expectations of the workers. It has been found necessary to call up new, self-governing trade unions which will become authentic representatives of the working class.

The government undertakes to submit to Parliament within three months a bill to revise the censorship laws, free public access to certain administrative documents . . . to permit the broadcasting of Catholic church services on Sundays . . . to submit for reconsideration by the ministry of justice the cases of named persons convicted in connection with human rights activities . . . wage increases for lower paid workers, increased provision of housing and pension facilities . . . The question of meat sales from commercial shops is to be examined."

Document questions

1 *Read Document* A.
  a Explain in your own words *two* ways in which the strikers felt that they didn't have enough freedom.
  b Look at the other demands in Document A and explain in your own words two other 'economic' reasons why the strikers felt that they needed a trade union.

2 *Read Document* B.
  a What excuse did Mr Babiuch give to explain why food prices had been put up?
  b Quote the phrase from Document B which suggests that Mr Babiuch didn't want to admit that the workers were on strike.
  c What doubts might the historian of Solidarity have in using TV interviews (as in Document B) as evidence?

3 *Look at Document* C.
  a Name the Soviet leader whose face is shown at the top of the cartoon.
  b Do you think the cartoonist is sympathetic towards the demands of the strikers or not? Explain your answer and describe what the cartoon shows.

4 *Look at the evidence in the documents.* Write sentences to explain four ways in which you think the government had kept the workers in order and under control between 1970 and 1980.

5 According to the evidence in the documents (see especially Document D), does the 'Solidarity strike' in 1980 appear to have been successful? Give three reasons for your answer.

Follow-on questions

6 *Look at Documents* A *and* D *again.* What do you think were the most important differences between Solidarity and a 'Western' trade union? Think of what the strikers were demanding and what they got.

7 Who was the leader of the strikers? What action did the Polish government later take against him?

8 Document D mentions the Catholic church. Why do you think the Catholic church is mentioned in a communist country?

9 Compare these documents with those about the Czechoslovakian crisis in 1968 (page 46). How did Soviet policy towards these two 'threats' differ? Why might it have been different?

3.1 The beginnings of the cold war

A Soviet cartoon, 1943. The translation is 'Merciless Rout and Annihilation of the Enemy'. The paper is 'The Treaty of Non-aggression between the USSR and Germany'.

B Soviet cartoon, 1943, entitled 'The Transformation of Fritz'.

C US Department of State memorandum: 'The Threat of International Communism to Europe and the United States', June 2 1945.
"To a communist, Europe today politically and economically represents a perfect situation. Europe is emerging from probably the most devastating war in its history. The Red Army's exploits have been so well advertised that the majority of Europeans regard them as their liberators. Even in the West the Red Army receives the lion's share of the credit, thanks to the publicity given it by the communist press. The excesses of the Nazi regime and the fear of a rejuvenated Germany force most Europeans to gravitate toward the strongest remaining power in Europe – the Soviet Union."

D From a speech by Soviet Foreign Minister V. M. Molotov at the Paris Peace Conference, October 10 1946.
"It cannot be said that the USA is one of those states which suffered serious material damage in the war. We are glad this did not happen to our ally, though we ourselves have had to go through trying times, the results of which will take us long years to heal.

Now that you know the facts, place side by side Romania, weakened by the war. It (USA) would buy up the local industries, take over the more attractive Romanian, Yugoslav and other businesses, and become masters in these small countries. It would, in practice, mean the economic enslavement of the small countries and their rule by strong, rich foreign firms, banks and industrial companies. Was this what we fought for when we battled against the fascist invaders, the Hitlerite and Japanese imperialists?"

Document questions

1 *Look at Document* [A].
  a Who is the 'creature' on the left supposed to be?
  b What is the piece of paper on the left of the poster and why is it shown as torn?

2 *Look at Document* [B].
  a Describe what you see in Document [B] and mention the clue in the poster that helps explain why the Nazi war effort failed.
  b The same Soviet artist drew Documents [A] and [B]. Write a few sentences to explain what he wanted people who saw the posters to think about the Nazis. Mention things from each poster to support your answer.

3 Compare the way the Red Army is shown in Document [A] and described in Document [C]. What similarity do you notice? Refer to both documents in your answer.

4 *Read Documents* [C] *and* [D]. List four reasons suggested in these documents why the USSR perhaps stood a better chance than the USA of gaining more power and influence in Europe at the end of the war. Write in your own words, rather than copying exactly from the documents.

5 What problems might there be for the historian of the cold war in using political speeches (as in Document [D]) as evidence?

Follow-on questions

6 What were the terms of the treaty shown in Document [A]? Why do you think it was such an important treaty?

7 Compare Documents [A] and [B] with the first world war posters (page 22). What similarity do you notice in the way the 'enemy' is shown?

3.2   The iron curtain

A **From a speech by Winston Churchill at Fulton, Missouri, March 5 1946.**
"From Stettin in the Baltic to Trieste in the Adriatic, an iron curtain has descended across the Continent. Behind that line lie all the capitals of the ancient states of central and eastern Europe, Warsaw, Berlin, Prague, Vienna, Budapest, Belgrade, Bucharest and Sofia, all these famous cities and the populations around them lie in the Soviet sphere and all are subject, in one form or another, not only to Soviet influence but to a very high and increasing measure of control from Moscow. (Athens, alone, with its immortal glories, is free to decide its future at an election under British, American and French observation.)

However, in a great number of countries, far from the Russian frontiers and throughout the world, communist fifth columns are established and work in complete unity and absolute obedience to the directions they receive from the communist centre. Except in the British Commonwealth and in the United States, where communism is in its infancy, the communist parties or fifth columns constitute a growing challenge and danger to Christian civilization."

B **'A Peep Under the Iron Curtain', a British cartoon 1946.**

C **Interview given by Josef Stalin, March 13 1946.**
"Hitler began his work of unleashing war by proclaiming a 'race theory', declaring that only German-speaking people constituted a superior nation. Mr Churchill sets out to unleash a war with a race theory, asserting that only English-speaking nations are superior nations, who are called upon to decide the destinies of the entire world. (And an ultimatum. Accept our rule voluntarily and then all will be well; otherwise war is inevitable.)

There can be no doubt that Mr Churchill's position is a call for a war on the USSR.

It is absurd to speak of exclusive control by the USSR in Vienna and Berlin, where there are allied control councils made up of the representatives of four states and where the USSR has only one-quarter of the votes.

The Soviet Union's loss of life (in the war) has been several times greater than that of Britain and the USA put together. Possibly in some quarters an inclination is felt to forget about these colossal sacrifices of the Soviet people which secured the liberation of Europe from the Hitlerite yoke. But the Soviet Union cannot forget about them. And so what can there be surprising about the fact that the Soviet Union, anxious for its future safety, is trying to see to it that governments loyal in their attitude to the Soviet Union should exist in these countries?"

D Soviet cartoon, 1948, entitled 'The Relay'.

Document questions

1 a According to Document Ⓐ, which country was to blame for the setting up of the 'iron curtain'?
  b Write a sentence to explain what you think the 'iron curtain' was.

2 *Look at Document Ⓑ.*
  a Who is 'Joe' on the wall?
  b How does the cartoon show Churchill's idea about an 'iron curtain'?
  c Describe what you see in the cartoon and quote a sentence from Document Ⓐ which you think the cartoon describes.

3 a Name one accusation made by Churchill about the Soviet Union in Document Ⓐ, and quote a line from Document Ⓒ to show how Stalin replied to that allegation.
  b How does Stalin justify in Document Ⓒ what appeared to be a Soviet takeover of Eastern Europe at the end of the second world war?

4 a Name any four of the people shown in Document Ⓓ.
  b Tell the story shown in Document Ⓓ and explain how it shows Stalin's ideas about Churchill. Back this up with a quotation from Document Ⓒ.

5 From what you know about the second world war, write a couple of sentences to explain two reasons why Churchill might have been particularly angry about the ideas suggested in Document Ⓓ.

6 What are the advantages and disadvantages to the historian of the iron curtain in using interviews (as in Document Ⓒ) as evidence?

Follow-on questions

7 In what way did Document Ⓑ predict an event that took place in 1961?

8 In what way might Document Ⓓ be described as 'propaganda'?

3.3   The U2 crisis

A **Statement by Nikita Khrushchev, Leader of the Soviet Union, May 16 1960.**
"On May 1 a US military reconnaissance aircraft invaded the Soviet Union while executing a specific espionage mission to obtain information on military and industrial installations on the territory of the USSR. After the aggressive purpose of its flight became known the aircraft was shot down by units of the Soviet rocket forces. Unfortunately, this has not been the only case of aggressive and espionage actions by the US air force against the Soviet Union. This means that if the US government is really ready to co-operate with the governments of the other powers in the interests of maintaining peace and strengthening confidence between states it must, first, condemn the inadmissible, provocative actions of the US air force with regard to the Soviet Union; and secondly, refrain from continuing such actions and such a policy against the USSR in the future.

Until this is done, the Soviet government sees no possibility for fruitful negotiations with the US government at the summit conference. It cannot be among the participants in negotiations where one of the parties has made treachery the basis of its policy with regard to the Soviet Union."

B **Statement by American President Dwight Eisenhower, May 16 1960.**
"The position of the United States was made clear with respect to the distasteful necessity of espionage activities in a world where nations distrust each other's intentions. We pointed out that these activities had no aggressive intent but rather were to assure the safety of the United States and the free world against surprise attack by a power which boasts of its ability to devastate the USA and other countries by missiles. Most other countries are constantly the targets of elaborate and persistent espionage of the Soviet Union . . .

These (reconnaissance overflights) were suspended after the recent incident and are not to be resumed. I have come to Paris to seek agreements with the Soviet Union which would eliminate the necessity for all forms of espionage, including overflights. I see no reason to use this incident to disrupt the conference.

My words were seconded and supported by my Western colleagues, who also urged Mr Khruschev to pursue the path of reason and common sense and to forget propaganda.

Mr Khrushchev brushed aside all arguments of reason, he came all the way from Moscow to Paris with the sole intention of sabotaging this meeting on which so much of the hopes of the world have rested."

C **British cartoon, May 1960.**

Document questions

1 a *Compare Documents* [A] *and* [B]. What difference do you notice in the way in which these two documents describe the aim, or purpose, of the 'U2 program'? Explain your answer and support it with quotations from Documents [A] and [B].

  b Why do you think Eisenhower was keen to announce that the USA had suspended U2 flights? Support your answer with a quotation.

2 *Look at Document* [C].

  a Of what are the dove and olive branch symbols?
  b Who are the men looking at the plane and dove?
  c What is the point the cartoonist is trying to make?

3 Suggest one way in which the U2 crisis might be seen as a propaganda victory for

  a The USSR, and
  b The USA.

Follow-on questions

4 Compare Documents [A] and [B] with those on the Korean war (pages 34–35). What similarity do you notice in the way in which the USA and the USSR described each others worldwide plans?

5 Apart from the U2 incident what other disagreements did the USA and USSR have in 1960?

6 What important military position did Dwight Eisenhower (Document [B]) hold during World War 2?

3.4   Cuban missile crisis

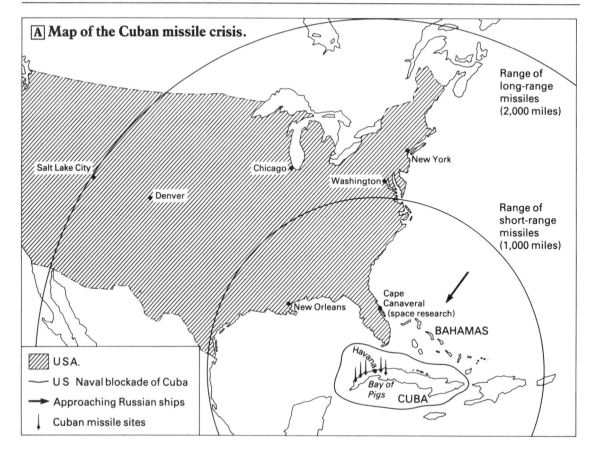

A Map of the Cuban missile crisis.

Range of long-range missiles (2,000 miles)

Range of short-range missiles (1,000 miles)

Salt Lake City

Denver

Chicago

New York

Washington

New Orleans

Cape Canaveral (space research)

BAHAMAS

Havana

Bay of Pigs   CUBA

U.S.A.

U S Naval blockade of Cuba

Approaching Russian ships

Cuban missile sites

B An English view of the Cuban missile crisis from 'World History in the 20th Century', by R. D. Cornwell, 1969.
"In 1958, Fidel Castro, a left-wing nationalist, came to power in Cuba. A series of radical measures led to opponents of his regime going to the US. In April 1961 these Cuban refugees invaded Cuba with the open moral support of Kennedy's government, and were completely defeated in the Bay of Pigs. Thereafter Castro declared himself a communist and received considerable military and economic aid from the communist bloc. In 1962 the US discovered and photographed a number of offensive surface-to-surface missile bases in Cuba. These communist missile bases represented a major threat to American security. Kennedy, therefore, ordered an American naval blockade of Cuba. For a few days the world seemed on the verge of a major nuclear war. But Khrushchev gave way: he agreed to the withdrawal of the missiles and the dismantling of the bases."

C A Soviet view of the Cuban missile crisis from 'Khrushchev Remembers', the memoirs of Soviet Leader Nikita Khrushchev.
"After Castro's crushing victory over the counter-revolutionaries, we intensified our military aid to Cuba . . . we were quite sure that the Americans would never get used to the existence of Castro's Cuba. They feared, as much as we hoped, that a socialist Cuba might become a magnet that would attract other Latin American countries to socialism . . . The fate of Cuba and the maintenance of Soviet prestige in that part of the world preoccupied me . . . We had to find a way of

stopping American interference in the Caribbean . . . The logical answer was missiles . . . I had the idea of installing missiles with nuclear warheads in Cuba without letting the United States find out they were there until it was too late to do anything about them . . . We had no desire to start a war . . .

. . . We sent the Americans a note saying that we agreed to remove our missiles and bombers on the condition that the President give us his assurance that there would be no invasion of Cuba by the forces of the United States or anybody else. Finally Kennedy gave in and agreed to make a statement giving us such an assurance . . . It was a great victory for us though . . . a spectacular success without having to fire a single shot!''

Document questions

1 *Look at Cuba's geographical position, shown in Document* A.
   a Even before the missiles were put on Cuba, why might the USA be particularly interested in what happened in Cuba?
   b How does Document A help explain why the United States government was so worried about the setting up of missiles on Cuba?

2 *Look at Documents* A *and* B.
   What was the 'US naval blockade of Cuba' and why did Kennedy order it?

3 Who were the 'counter-revolutionaries' mentioned in Document C?

4 *Compare Documents* B *and* C. What differences do you notice in the way in which these documents describe
   a why the crisis began, and
   b why the crisis ended?
   Support your answers with quotations.

5 Why do you think Documents B and C give such different versions of the crisis?

Follow-on questions

6 What were the 'radical measures' mentioned in Document B?
7 Why do you think the Cuban missile crisis was such an important event in the history of the cold war?

4.1 Hitler's rise to power

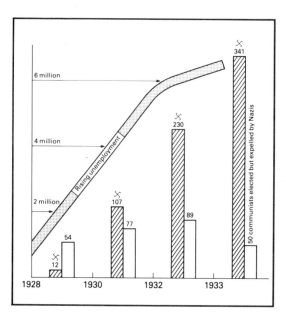

A Diagram showing the relationship between unemployment and the numbers of seats held by Nazis and communists in the German parliament 1928–33

B Some of the most important points in the Nazi manifesto

1) We demand the union of all Germans to form a Great Germany.
2) We demand equal rights for the German people in its dealings with other nations. We demand the abolition of the Treaty of Versailles.
3) We demand land for the resettlement of our surplus population.
4) Only members of the nation may be members of the German state. Only those of German blood may be citizens. Therefore, no Jew may be a member of the nation.
5) Only German citizens are allowed to vote.
6) All non-German immigration must be stopped. The workers must have more say in the running of industry.
7) We demand better old age pensions.
8) We demand punishment by death for moneylenders and others who have profited from the war.
9) We demand that all newspaper editors be members of the German nation. Non Germans must not take part in or influence German newspapers.
10) We demand a strong central government.

C Photograph taken at a Nazi rally.

D **Extract from 'Adolf Hitler' by John Toland, 1976.**
"Hitler offered something to almost every German voter in 1930 – the farmer, the worker, the student, the patriot, the racist and the middle-class burgher. The common denominator of his wide appeal was the world depression. Hitler's appeal to workers was couched in communist terminology. 'Working Germany, awake! Break your chains in two!' To farmers, Hitler offered tax adjustments and import duties. The lower middle class were offered hope: to the young, an idealistic new world. This last group listened entranced as he preached against selfishness and promised to establish social justice. Convinced that Hitler would create a genuine socialist government these young people roamed the streets of the large cities chanting the slogan they shared with their communist enemies, 'freedom, work and bread!'. In 1930 he was offering Germans something new – a feeling of unity, he welcomed everyone to join in his fight to the death against the Jews and the Reds, in his struggle for Lebensraum and the glory and the good of Germany."

Document questions

1 *Look at Document* A. In which year did unemployment reach its height in Germany?

2 Do you think the issue of unemployment was an important factor in helping to explain Hitler's rise to power? Quote evidence from Document A to support your answer.

3 Quote a sentence from Document B that you think might have appealed to
   a 'the worker',
   b 'the patriot', and
   c 'the racist'.
   Remember also to write a sentence explaining each part of the answer.

4 a What is a manifesto (Document B)?
   b Why do you think Hitler had so many different ideas in the Nazi manifesto (Document B)?

5 Describe carefully what you see in Document C. How do the things seen in the photograph help explain why so many people were attracted to Hitler's Nazi party?

6 Some photographs of Nazi rallies were called 'propaganda' photographs. What does this mean, and what doubts might the historian of Nazi Germany have in using propaganda photographs as evidence?

Follow-on questions

7 How important do you think the Treaty of Versailles was in explaining Hitler's rise to power? Support your answer by referring to the terms of the treaty.

8 *Read Document* D. Look at the two slogans quoted in this document which appealed to the 'workers' and the 'young idealists'. From which political party does Hitler seem to have borrowed these ideas?

9 In a paragraph explain what you think we learn from these documents about Hitler's qualities as a leader. Support your answer with quotations from the documents.

4.2 The night of the long knives

A From 'The Diary of Alfred Rosenberg', June 30 1934.
"With an SS escort detachment the Fuehrer drove to Wiessee and knocked gently on Roehm's door: 'A message from Munich', he said in a disguised voice. 'Well, come in', Roehm shouted to the supposed messenger, 'the door is open'. Hitler tore open the door, fell on Roehm as he lay in bed, packed him by the throat and screamed, 'You are under arrest, you pig!' Then he turned the traitor over to the SS.

Amann said, 'The biggest pig must go'. And to Hess: 'I'll shoot Roehm myself'. Hess replied, 'No it's my responsibility, even if I'd be shot for it afterwards'. Roehm was shot to death in his cell."

Photographer : " The last photograph, sir. **Kindly look this way, please.**"
(*The British Legion delegation arrive home today*)

B British cartoon, July 1934.

C From 'The Third Reich' by Michael Berwick, 1971.
"Even the fate of Ernst Roehm was the subject of some jealous haggling. Rudolf Hess and Max Amann, the Nazi Party publisher, both wanted the job. 'My Fuehrer, the duty to shoot Roehm is mine', Hess is reported to have said. Six SA leaders were cold-bloodedly shot on Hitler's orders in Stadelheim Jail. Dr Wilhelm Schmid was taken by the SS and a coffin sent to his family some time later from Dachau concentration camp with the order that it was to remain closed. The savaged body of Ritter von Kahr was found on open country near Dachau, mutilated by a pick-axe. General von Schleicher was gunned down at his office desk, and so was his wife. Roehm himself was shot three times in his cell and killed.

The total number of murders will probably never be known. It was the first act of wanton barbarism of the third Reich. It underlined the bloody character of Hitler's dictatorship, since now he could dispense with legality. In a speech in the Reichstag on July 13 1934, he said: 'If anyone reproaches me and asks why I did not resort to the regular courts of justice then all I can say is this: in this hour I was responsible for the fate of the German people and thereby I became the supreme judge of the German people'."

D British cartoon, July 1934.

THEY SALUTE WITH BOTH HANDS NOW

Hitler   Göbbels   Göring

Document questions

1 *Read Document* A.
  a Who was Roehm?
  b How does Document A help us to understand how unreliable diaries can be as a source of evidence to the historian?

2 *Compare Documents* A *and* C. Name two things both documents said happened that night.

3 Which of the documents might most accurately be described as a secondary source? Explain your answer.

4 Name the two other Nazi leaders, apart from Hitler, who can be seen in Documents B and D. Say what jobs these men had in the Nazi government.

5 Describe what you see happening in Document D. What point do you think the cartoonist is trying to make?

6 What reason did Hitler give in Document C for not using 'the regular courts of Justice'?

7 Document C mentions the 'bloody character of Hitler's dictatorship'. What other evidence of this bloody dictatorship can you see in Document B?

Follow-on questions

8 Who was Hess (Document A)?

9 Suggest reasons why Hitler took action against the SA leaders.

10 Who were the SA and the SS (Document C)?

11 What was the 'Reichstag' (Document C)?

4.3 Nazi education

A **From the Nazi educationalist, Hans Schemm: 'His Speeches and His Work', 1935.**

"The goal of our education is formation of character. We don't intend to educate our children into becoming miniature scholars. Therefore I say: let us have, rather, ten pounds less knowledge and ten calories more character."

B **From 'Other Men's Graves' by Peter Neumann, 1958.**

"I had no lectures that afternoon. When Klauss got back from school at 5 he bullied me into helping him with his homework. Glancing through his schoolbooks, I noticed again how different they were from those I had had only a few years ago.

Here is a maths problem, selected at random:

'A sturmkampfflieger on take-off carried twelve dozen bombs, each weighing ten kilos. The aircraft makes for Warsaw, the centre of international jewry. It bombs the town. On take-off with all the bombs on board and a fuel tank containing 1,500 kilos of fuel, the aircraft weighed about 8 tons. When it returned from the crusade, there are still 230 kilos of fuel left. What is the weight of the aircraft when empty?'

Here is another question that I had to solve for Klauss:

'The iniquitous Treaty of Versailles, imposed by the French and the English, enabled international plutocracy to steal Germany's colonies. France herself got part of Togoland. If German Togoland, temporarily under the administration of the French imperialists, covers 56 million square kilometres, and contains a population of 800,000 people, estimate the average living space per inhabitant.'"

C **Pictures taken from 'Trust No Fox and No Jew', a Nazi publication.**

D From a Nazi children's colouring book.
  (The text is in translation).

My Leader!

(The child speaks:)
I know you well and love you
          like father and mother
I intend to obey you always
          like father and mother
And when I am grown up, I shall help you
          like father and mother
And you should be proud of me
          like father and mother

Document questions

1 According to Document A, what was the aim of Nazi education? Write a couple of sentences to explain what you think was so extraordinary about this aim.

2 *Read Document* B. What was so unusual about the 'sturmkampfflieger' maths problem? Explain your answer and back it up with a quotation from this maths problem.

3 Name the two racial groups of people shown in Document C. Describe carefully how these two racial groups are shown in the pictures – how they can be identified.

4 What do you think the Nazis wanted children who saw Documents C and D to think? Explain your answer.

5 From looking at the documents, what would you assume that the education system in Germany had been like before the Nazis came to power?

Follow-on questions

6 How does the aim of Nazi education, expressed in Document A, help to explain what was studied in lessons in Nazi schools?

7 Why do you think physical fitness was such an important part of Nazi education?

8 Write a sentence to explain why you think the Nazis included each of these in the second maths problem in Document B:
   a the Treaty of Versailles,
   b German Togoland, and
   c living space.

4.4 Cult of personality

A Speech by Hitler to Nazi party members, August 1933.
"The most important part of fascism is absolute trust in a wise and able leader. Unless the nation completely trusts this one man it cannot be reconstructed. Therefore the leader will naturally be a great person, so that he serves as a model for all party members. Each member must sacrifice everything, acting directly for the leader and the group and indirectly for society, the nation and the revolution."

B From 'Mussolini' by Denis Mack Smith, 1981.
"The years after 1926 saw an ever increasing spread of the legend of an all-wise Duce, and this cult of Ducismo was the most effective feature of fascism. Mussolini encouraged it not just out of vanity but as an instrument of power. The ministers of the faith were the other leading fascists who all realised that their future depended on his. Without him they were nothing: the greater he was, the greater would they be. He was called the greatest genius in Italian history and corrected the pages of his biography. Fascism was seen as his personal creation, as something that, without submission to him, would cease to exist."

C From 'Stalin: a Political Biography' by Isaac Deutscher, 1949.
"The 'cult of his personality' assumed absurd forms. He was addressed as father of the peoples, the greatest genius in history, shining sun of humanity. According to Khrushchev, 'Stalin used all methods to glorify himself. He edited an official account of his own life which included this phrase: "Stalin never allowed his work to be marred by the slightest hint of vanity, conceit or self adulation".' Like a drug addict he craved the incense burnt for him. He seemed to be still trying to escape from the sense of inferiority that had so long gnawed at him."

D Official Nazi party photograph of Hitler and the SA men.

E Official
photograph of
Mussolini
cutting corn.

F Official
photograph of
Stalin.

Document questions

1 *Read Documents* A *and* B. Carefully explain in your own words two reasons why a strong leader was thought to be so important in a fascist country. Support your answer with a quotation from Document A.

2 *Read Documents* B *and* C.
  a Name two similarities in the things Mussolini and Stalin did. You don't have to quote, just write a couple of sentences describing two things they both did.
  b Suggest two reasons why Mussolini and Stalin did these things. Explain your answer carefully.

3 *Look at the three pictures (Documents* D–F*).* Each was produced for a reason. According to the pictures, what was each of the dictators like? What 'image' of themselves do you think they were trying to put across and why did they want to be shown in this way? Write your answers under the headings: i) Hitler, ii) Mussolini and iii) Stalin.

4 What problems might there be for the historian of the cult of personality in using a political biography (as in Document C) as evidence?

Follow-on questions

5 *Read Documents* B *and* C.
  a Which parts of the 'cult of personality' seem a little ridiculous today and why?
  b Why do you think the people in Mussolini's government encouraged and carried out even the more ridiculous parts of the 'cult of personality'? Support your answer with a quotation from Document B.

6 *Read Document* C.
  a What do we learn about Stalin's personality? Support your answer with quotations.
  b From reading Documents A and B, do you think Mussolini's and Hitler's personalities were at all similar to Stalin's? Support your answer with a quotation from Document A and a quotation from Document B.

7 From what you know about the political history of Italy and the USSR suggest a reason why it might be thought surprising that Mussolini and Stalin did such similar things. Write a couple of sentences to explain your answer.

5.1   Britain and Abyssinia

A **From 'Facing the Dictators', the autobiography of Anthony Eden (British Foreign Secretary at the time of the Abyssinian Crisis), 1962.**
"I reported the government's opinion that the best action to take would be the prohibition of the import of Italian goods. The object of this ban was to deprive Italy of a large part of her power to buy goods abroad. If all members of the league applied this embargo, 70 per cent of Italy's export trade would be cut off. Britain now had taken a decision, as one of fifty nations, to try to stop Mussolini."

THE AWFUL WARNING.

FRANCE AND ENGLAND *(together ?).* "WE DON'T WANT YOU TO FIGHT, BUT, BY JINGO, IF YOU DO, WE SHALL PROBABLY ISSUE A JOINT MEMORANDUM SUGGESTING A MILD DISAPPROVAL OF YOU."

B **Cartoon from *Punch*, 1935.**

C **From 'Italian Fascism' by Giampiero Carocci, 1972.**
"In spite of opposition, led by Britain in the League of Nations, Mussolini got everything he wanted: Ethiopia and the Empire. But the most important of the economic sanctions, the one on petrol, was not applied, nor was the Suez Canal closed to Italian ships.

The British government wished to avoid war with Italy at all costs because of the weakness of the British navy after years of disarmament. This weakness made such a war seem completely out of the question. Although the British would certainly have won, they would have had to fight without military support from France, and would have been further weakened in the face of two other threats, considered far more serious: Japan and Germany. Through his secret services Mussolini knew how weak the British navy had become and he exploited this knowledge to the full."

D **From 'Mussolini' by Denis Mack Smith, 1981.**
"For several years Mussolini had been intercepting communications through the French and British embassies in Rome, and must have had confirmation from this source that there was a firm determination not to risk war against Italy at almost any cost. When in June the British proposed a negotiated settlement over Ethiopia, he did not think it need be taken seriously. British rearmament had barely started and he would have known that there was a secret commitment in London to giving priority to the Japanese threat in the Far East."

Document questions

1 By what other name is Abyssinia known in these documents?

2 a Explain what an 'embargo' is and how it was thought that it would stop Mussolini.
  b Explain one weakness of the League of Nations that is suggested in Document [A], and back it up with a quotation from the document.

3 *Look at Document* [B].
  a Name the person seen standing on the right hand side of the cartoon.
  b Do you think that the person who drew the cartoon was probably a supporter or an opponent of the British government's policy on Abyssinia? Support your answer by mentioning things from the cartoon.

4 *Read Document* [C].
  a Why do you think it was so important to have economic sanctions on petrol?
  b Suggest a reason why economic sanctions on petrol were not applied.
  c Where is the 'Suez Canal' and why was it so important to close it to Italian ships?

5 *Compare Documents* [C] *and* [D]. Name two things that both of these documents agree on.

6 Was the Abyssinian crisis a success or a failure for the British government? Give reasons for your answer, and quote from the documents.

Follow-on questions

7 What were the main causes of the Abyssinian crisis?

8 Why did Anthony Eden resign as Foreign Secretary (Document [A])?

5.2 Rhineland

A **From 'Adolf Hitler' by John Toland, 1976.**
"'The forty-eight hours after the march into the Rhineland', he told his interpreter, 'were the most nerve-racking in my life'. If the French had retaliated 'we would have had to withdraw with our tails between our legs, for the military resources at our disposal would have been wholly inadequate for even a moderate resistance.'"

B **From 'Diaries and Letters, 1930–39' by Harold Nicolson, 1966.**
"We know that Hitler gambled on this coup. Thus if we send an ultimatum to Germany she ought in all reason to climb down. Naturally we shall win and enter Berlin. But what is the good of that? It would only mean communism in Germany and France, and that is why the Russians are so keen on it. Moreover the people of this country absolutely refuse to have a war. We should be faced by a general strike if we even suggested such a thing. We shall therefore have to climb down ignominiously and Hitler will have scored. We must swallow this humiliation as best we may, and be prepared to become the laughing stock of Europe. It means the final end of the League."

THE GOOSE-STEP.
"GOOSEY GOOSEY GANDER,
WHITHER DOST THOU WANDER!"
"ONLY THROUGH THE RHINELAND—
PRAY EXCUSE MY BLUNDER!"

C **British cartoon, 1936.**

Document questions

1 *Read Documents* A *and* B.
   a Was Hitler taking a risk in marching into the Rhineland? Write a sentence to explain your answer and back it up with quotations from Documents A and B.
   b How useful to the historian of the Rhineland crisis is a biography of Hitler (as in Document A) as evidence?
   c Suggest two reasons given by the writer in Document B to explain why he thought Britain could not go to war with Germany over the Rhineland crisis.

2 *Look at Document* C. Explain carefully why you think the cartoonist has included the following things and what they mean:
   a the weapons,
   b the flags,
   c the olive branch with 'Pax Germanica' on it and
   d the title 'the goose step' and the poem beneath it.

3 Use the information in the documents to explain whether you think the Rhineland crisis was a victory or defeat for Germany and/or for Britain.

Follow-on questions

4 Document C mentions 'Locarno'. What was Locarno and why was it important?

5 Compare these documents with those on appeasement (page 70). What similarity in British policy do you notice?

5.3 Appeasement

STILL HOPE

A British cartoon from *Punch*, September 21 1938.

B Transcript from *The Daily Express*, September 30 1938.
PEACE

Be glad in your hearts. Give thanks to your God.
The wings of peace settle about us and the peoples of Europe. The prayers of the troubled hearts are answered.
People of Britain, your children are safe. Your husbands and your sons will not march to battle.

A war which would have been the most criminal, the most futile, the most destructive that ever insulted the purposes of the Almighty and the intelligence of men has been averted.

It was the war that nobody wanted. Nobody in Germany. Nobody in France. Nobody, above all, in Britain, which had no concern whatever with the issues at stake.

To him the laurels.

If we must have a victor, let us choose Chamberlain. For the prime minister's conquests are mighty and enduring – millions of happy homes and hearts relieved of their burden. To him the laurels!

C From J. F. Kennedy's 'Why England Slept', 1962.
"(People) felt and many still do feel that Hitler in 1938 was merely bluffing . . .
    People felt that Chamberlain was badly taken in, but I think a study of the position of the two countries will show that Chamberlain was sincere in thinking that a great step had been taken towards healing one of Europe's fever sores. I believe that English public opinion was not sufficiently aroused to back him in a war. Most people in England felt: 'It's not worth a war to prevent the Sudeten Germans from going back to Germany'. They failed at that time to see the larger issue, involving the domination of Europe. But though all these factors played a part in the settlement of Munich, I feel that Munich was inevitable on the grounds of lack of armaments alone."

D British cartoon, October 1938.

"EUROPE CAN LOOK FORWARD TO A CHRISTMAS OF PEACE"—HITLER

Document questions

1 **a** Name the person shown in Document A.
 b Whom was he on his way to meet?

2 Does the author of Document C agree or disagree with what was said in Document B about public opinion in England? Explain your answer carefully, then support it with a quotation from Document B and one from Document C.

3 **a** Name the politician seen standing on the left of Document D.
 b Who are the 'babes' in the bed supposed to be?
 c Why are the 'babes' shown being bundled into Santa's sack?
 d Why do you think the cartoonist has included the words 'Europe can look forward to a Christmas of peace'?

4 Neville Chamberlain's policy towards Hitler has been called 'appeasement'.
 Using the evidence in the documents write a paragraph explaining why he followed this policy.

5 What are the advantages and disadvantages to the historian of appeasement in using newspapers (as in Document B) as evidence?

Follow-on questions

6 The author of Document C was an American. What important job did J. F. Kennedy hold between 1960 and 1963?

7 From Document D what steps did 'Santa' take after Munich and before September 1939 to fill his sack with even more of the 'babes' from the bed?

8 Write a reply to Document B. As the editor of a different British newspaper, write an article criticising Chamberlain's policy at Munich. Try to reply to each of the points made in Document B.

5.4 The Nazi–Soviet pact

A British cartoon, September 20 1939.

B From R. Payne's 'The Rise and Fall of Stalin', 1965.

"At one o'clock in the morning the non-aggression pact and the secret protocol were solemnly signed by Ribbentrop and Molotov. The protocol remained unknown in the West until after the war, when men had grown so accustomed to physical horrors that they could scarcely breathe a sigh for horrors committed on paper. The secret protocol was a diabolic document, for it ensured that Poland would be destroyed and that the war would extend across the whole earth. It could be regarded in the same light as a document signed by potential murderers on the subject of the disposal of corpses. Germany and Russia were not in friendly alliance, Stalin and Hitler were conspirators giving aid and comfort to one another as they both prepared to plunge their knives into Poland."

C A Soviet view of the pact.

"The treaty with Germany was a step which the USSR was forced to take in the difficult situation that had come about in the summer of 1939. The Soviet government did not deceive itself regarding Hitler's aims. It understood that the treaty would not bring the USSR lasting peace but only a more or less lengthy breathing-space. When it signed the treaty with Germany the Soviet government undertook the task of using the time thus gained to carry through the political and military measures needed in order to ensure the country's security and strengthen its capacity for defence."

Document questions

1 **a** Name the two men shown on either side of Document [A].
   b Give the name of the country you think the dead body in the middle of Document [A] is supposed to be.
   c Quote the line from Document [B] which you think helps tell you which country the dead body in Document [A] is.

2 Document [B] mentions a 'non aggression pact'. Write a sentence to explain what you think a non aggression pact is.

3 Write a couple of sentences to explain why it was surprising that the two men shown standing in Document [A] should make a non aggression pact with each other.

4 Write a sentence to explain what you think a 'secret protocol' is (Document [B]).

5 *Compare Documents* [A] *and* [B]. Do you think the author of Document [B] would agree or disagree with the cartoonist's opinion about the Nazi–Soviet pact? Quote from both documents to support your answer.

6 **a** Quote the line from Document [C] that gives a reason why the USSR made the pact with Germany.
   b Look at the answer you've just written (**a**). How is this reason you quoted different from that given in Document [B]?
   c Why do you think Documents [B] and [C] tell such different stories? Write a few sentences. Think of what the documents are.
   d How does Document [C] help us to understand why we must be careful about using Document [B] as evidence?

Follow-on questions

7 With which other country had the USSR been discussing an agreement in the summer of 1939? Suggest reasons why Stalin decided not to make an agreement with that country.

8 Suggest two advantages or benefits for Germany and two disadvantages or risks in signing the pact with the USSR.

6.1 Dunkirk

A **From 'World War II – Dunkirk', edited by Brigadier Peter Young, 1972.**
"Despite the undoubted setback represented by the allied evacuations from Dunkirk, Hitler had scored a crushing victory. For German losses put at 10,252 killed, 42,523 wounded and 8,467 missing, he announced that 1,212,000 Dutch, Belgian, French and British prisoners had been taken. In addition, his armies had captured an enormous booty: from the British army alone, the spoils taken by the Germans amounted to 1,200 field guns, 1,250 anti-aircraft and anti-tank guns, 11,000 machine guns and 75,000 vehicles. It is not surprising, therefore, that his letters to Mussolini were flushed with optimism."

B **From 'Cartoonists at War' by Frank Huggett, 1981.**
"What could have been the greatest military defeat in British history was turned into a victory by British ingenuity, pragmatism and pluck, Hitler's irresolution, and Goering's false boasts that his Luftwaffe could eliminate the BEF while it waited on the beaches. The British, always at their best when they are staring real disaster firmly in the face, were united in their defence. Not for the first time in its history, Britain stood alone."

C **British cartoon, May 29 1940.**

D **Statement in the *Green Howards Gazette*, November 1962, by General Sir Harold Franklyn, divisional commander at Dunkirk.**
"The evacuation has been overglamourised. Reports of 'merciless bombing' and 'the hell of Dunkirk' were ridiculous. I walked along the beaches on several occasions and never saw a corpse; there was very little shelling. As for cowardice in every unit there are some men who have no stomach for the fight. There were instances of a few men embarking at Dunkirk when their battalions were fighting near the canal."

Document questions

1 According to Document [A], which side gained victory at Dunkirk? Write a sentence to explain your answer, then back it up with a quotation from the Document.

2 **a** *Look at your answer to question* **1**, *then read Document* [B]. What difference do you notice? Support your explanation with a quotation from Document [B].
  b If Documents [A] and [B] say different things about what happened at Dunkirk, does that mean that one of these two documents must be lying? Look carefully again at what the two documents say and give a couple of reasons for your answer.

3 *Look at Document* [C]. Does it agree more with the ideas in Document [A], or those in Document [B]? Give a reason for your answer and explain carefully the point you think the cartoonist is trying to make.

4 Is Document [C] a primary source or a secondary source? Give a reason for your answer.

5 How useful to the historian of Dunkirk are cartoons (as in Document [C]) as evidence?

6 Document [D] is an eye-witness account of Dunkirk by a divisional commander. What are the advantages and disadvantages to the historian of Dunkirk of using Document [D] as evidence?

Follow-on questions

7 From what you know about the events of 1940 explain why you think that the evacuation of Dunkirk 'has been overglamourised'. Think about what happened at Dunkirk and why it was an important time for Britain. Try to make four points in your answer.

8 What part of the Dunkirk story do you think the author of Document [B] was referring to when he mentioned 'Hitler's irresolution'?

6.2 The bombing of Coventry

A From the *Daily Herald*, November 16 1940.

COVENTRY

THE bombing of Coventry was as foul a deed as even Hitler has ever ordained.

Clearly his airmen were instructed: "Don't worry if you cannot reach your industrial targets. Bomb and burn the city.

Never mind if you fail to hit factories. Hit houses.

Have no scruples about military objectives. Kill men, kill women, kill children.

Destroy! Destroy! Destroy!

Heil Hitler! Heil bloodshed! Heil pain!

The Orgy

ANTI-AIRCRAFT fire, the Ministry of Home Security's communiqué tells us, hindered accurate bombing of industrial targets.

So the orgy began.

Bombs by the thousand were poured on houses and churches, shops and hotels.

Squadron after squadron dived upon the helpless city.

It was, chortled the Berlin propagandist yesterday afternoon, "the greatest attack in the history of air warfare."

And what has it achieved?

It has proved once again the calm courage of ordinary British people in this hell of Hitler's making.

It has fortified their resolve to fight him, to smash him, to strive and struggle without pause until the Nazi nightmare is nothing more than a sickening memory.

B A Broadcast from Berlin radio, November 16 1940.

"More than 500 planes took part in the greatest attack in the history of aerial warfare. About 500 tons of high explosive bombs and 30,000 incendiary bombs were dropped. In a short time all large and small factories were set on fire. The German air force struck a violent blow in return for the failed British raid on the Nazi Party celebrations in Munich on the night of November 8.

Coventry – the centre of the British aircraft industry – was raided by waves of strong forces of German bombers. The defences were helpless against the vigorous attack of the Luftwaffe. Numerous engine works and large plants of the aircraft accessory industry, as well as other plants of military importance were plastered with bombs, which caused tremendous devastation."

C Photograph of bomb damage from the *Coventry Evening Telegraph*, November 16 1940.

D From P. Knightley's 'The First Casualty', 1982.

"The people could not always take it. In fact the German attack created panic. Thousands fled from the town in an unorganised riot. The army wanted to impose martial law, and an official report described the general mood by repeating what a survivor said: 'Coventry is finished'. Coventry was actually a legitimate military target, one of the keys to the British war effort, and the German bombers damaged 21 important factories, including the Daimler motor works and the Alvis aero-engine factory. 'Here tools and motors were made for British aircraft', the German PK reporter who flew with the Luftwaffe on the attack quite accurately told his readers. The fact that the cathedral was hit and that industrial production in Coventry rose after the attack are two indictments of bombing as a weapon of war. Yet instead Coventry has gone down in history as a monument to German frightfulness."

Document questions

1 *Compare Documents A and B*. What difference do you notice in the explanations of
  a why the Germans had bombed Coventry, and
  b how successful the raid was?

2 Suggest one reason why the stories given in Documents A and B are so different. Explain your answer.

3 a What does Document C show and why might the British government have wanted this photograph published?
  b What kind of photograph might the Germans have wanted to publish?
  c Suggest one reason why photographs might be seen as an unreliable source of evidence about the bombing of Coventry. Explain your answer.

4 a Which parts of Document B are supported by Document D?
  b Which parts of Document B are shown by Document D to be untrue?

5 a What are the problems for the historian in using radio broadcasts (like Document B) as evidence?
  b What are the advantages to the historian in using radio broadcasts (like Document B) as evidence?

Follow-on questions

6 Write a few sentences to explain why it is so difficult to write a fair description of the bombing of Coventry.

7 Knightley's book (Document D) takes its title from the quotation 'Truth is the first casualty of war'. Write a paragraph to explain what you think this quotation means and give examples from the documents.

8 Draw two propaganda posters:
  a a British poster about the raid on Coventry. Show how the British government wanted people to react to the raid, and
  b a German poster about the raid on Coventry. Show how the German government wanted people to react to the raid.

6.3   World war two posters

A

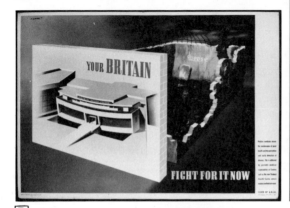

B

C

D

E

Document questions

1 *Compare Documents [A] and [B].*
  a What similarity do you notice in the message or ideas put forward in these two posters? Explain your answer and support it with a quotation from the posters.
  b What differences do you notice in the ways in which Documents [A] and [B] put forward their ideas?

2 a *Look at Document [D].* From what you know about Britain's changing relationship with Russia, write a few sentences to describe and explain what strikes you as interesting or unusual about the message written on this poster?
  b *Look at the women in Documents [C] and [D].* What difference do you notice in the image or appearance of the two women?

3 Document [C] was banned by the government and later replaced by Document [E]. Why do you think this happened? Carefully describe the way in which the women are shown in the two posters, and what you think the government wanted women to be like and why.

4 How valuable to the historian of the second world war are posters (like those shown here) as evidence?

Follow-on questions

5 *Compare Documents [C], [D] and [E] with the 'Women of Britain Say Go' poster shown in the section about first world war posters (page 22):* What similarities and differences do you notice in the way in which women were shown in posters in these two wars? Support your answer by mentioning things in the posters.

6 What do you think makes a good poster? Choose any two of the posters (from either war) and write a paragraph to explain why you think these posters are successful and effective.

6.4   'D' day – Overlord embroidery

A **From 'The Making of the Embroidery', 1984.**

"The Overlord Embroidery was commissioned in 1968 by Lord Dulverton as a tribute to, and a permanent memorial and record of, the effort made by the allies to liberate Europe during the 1939–45 war.

The Embroidery, which is unique, depicts the allied invasion of Normandy of 6th June, 1944. It traces the planning and historical detail of Operation Overlord from Britain's darkest hour in 1940 through to victory in the Battle of Normandy in August 1944.

The Embroidery consists of 34 panels, each 8 feet long and 3 feet high; measures 272 feet in length and is the largest work of its kind in the world. It is 41 feet longer than the 11th century Bayeux Tapestry, its counterpart.

The embroidery was designed by Miss Sandra Lawrence under the direction of a specially formed advisory committee, comprising 3 senior officers of the armed forces.

A scale drawing and subsequently full size cartoon of each panel was prepared by Miss Lawrence using many wartime photographs as reference material to ensure authenticity."

B Panel from the Overlord Embroidery '4th US Division Lands on Utah Beach'.

C Allied troops landing in Normandy, 6 June 1944.

D Panel from the Overlord Embroidery, showing the inspection of the invasion beaches with *Mulberry* in the background.

E Translation from an introduction to the Bayeux Tapestry.
"The Bayeux Tapestry, a historical record created in the 11th century, is the only masterpiece of its kind in the world.

It is an embroidery on a linen cloth using wools of various colours.

This (play on a stage) over 70 metres long and 50 centimetres high, retraces the history of the conquest of England by William the Conqueror."

Document questions

1 Do you think the Overlord embroidery is a primary source or a secondary source? Give a reason for your answer.

2 **a** What does Document **C** show and why might it be thought to be a more reliable source of evidence to the historian of D-day than Document **B**?
b If Document **B** is a less reliable source than Document **C**, does that mean that Document **B** is useless to the historian of D-day as evidence? Explain your answer and mention things from the documents.

3 *Look at Documents* **A** *and* **E**. Document **A** calls the embroidery 'the modern day counterpart' of the 11th century Bayeux tapestry. In a paragraph explain what this means and describe ways in which the tapestry and the embroidery are similar. Support your answer with quotations from the documents.

4 In what way might both the Bayeux tapestry and the Overlord embroidery be described as biased sources of evidence?

5 Name one primary source *not* mentioned in these documents that might be useful to the historian of D-day as evidence. Explain your answer carefully.

Follow-on questions

6 Name the King, the General and the Prime Minister numbered 1, 2, and 3 in Document **D**.

7 What part did PLUTO play in the D-day story?

8 Document **D** shows *Mulberry* in the background. What was *Mulberry* and why do you think it was so useful to the invaders?

6.5 Auschwitz

A **Notes from Hitler's adjutant, General Fritz Wiedemann, September 1935.**
"Hitler remarked: 'Out with the Jews from all the professions and into the ghetto with them; fence them in somewhere they can perish as they deserve while the German people look on, the way people stare at wild animals'."

B **'Polish Jew and Nazi Soldiers', a contemporary photograph.**

C **From the 'Memoirs of Rudolf Höss', first commandant of Auschwitz.**
"In the summer of 1941 I was suddenly summoned, Himmler said:

'The Führer has ordered the Jewish question to be solved once and for all and that we, the SS are to implement that order. The existing extermination centres in the east are not in a position to carry out the large actions that are anticipated. I have therefore earmarked Auschwitz for this purpose. You will treat this order as absolutely secret, even from your superiors. The Jews are the sworn enemies of the German people and must be eradicated. Every Jew that we can lay our hands on is to be destroyed now, during the war, without exception'."

D **Statement by Kazimierz Smolen, ex-prisoner of Auschwitz.**
"Auschwitz is not only the symbol of human agony and ruthless flaunting of human rights – it is also proof of the crime of genocide perpetrated by the fascist Hitlerites. It came to be the biggest centre of final extermination of the Jews brought from all the occupied countries of Europe. We are preserving this place as a testimony of the inferno which fascism prepared for the entire world, as a memento for generations to come. Here, trampled underfoot were human dignity and the right to existence even if one was of a different race or religion."

E Photograph taken after the liberation of
a concentration camp in Germany, 1945.

Document questions

1 What do you think the soldiers are doing to the Jew in Document **B** and why?

2 *Compare Documents* **A** *and* **B**. What similarity do you notice in the attitudes shown towards Jews? Explain your answer and mention things from both documents.

3 What are the advantages and disadvantages to the historian of Auschwitz in using the memoirs of Commandant Höss (Document **C**) as evidence?

4 Quote words from Document **C** which give evidence of the 'crime of genocide' mentioned in Document **D**. Explain your answer.

5 Describe what you see in Document **E** and explain why you think the German people were made to look at the cart.

6 Write a paragraph to explain how the Nazis justified the extermination of the Jews. Give at least two quotations in your answer.

Follow-on questions

7 By what name were the laws known which were passed in 1935 to get the Jews 'out from all the professions'?

8 What methods of extermination had been tried by the Nazis before the use of gas chambers? Why were these methods abandoned?

9 Write a paragraph to explain why you think the events at Auschwitz should never be forgotten.

10 Suggest reasons why the allies didn't do something to stop the suffering at Auschwitz until the end of the war.

6.6 Hiroshima

A **From the memoirs of President Harry Truman.**

"In all it had been estimated that it would require until the late fall of 1946 to bring Japan to her knees. All of us realized that the fighting would be fierce and the losses heavy. General Marshall told me that it might cost half a million American lives to force the enemy's surrender on his home ground.

We laboured to construct a weapon of such overpowering force that the enemy could be forced to yield swiftly once we could resort to it. I set up a committee of top men and asked them to study with great care the implications the new weapon might have for us. It was their recommendation that the bomb should be used against the enemy as soon as it could be done.

I regarded the bomb as a military weapon and never had any doubt that it should be used. In deciding to use this bomb I wanted to make sure that it would be used in a manner prescribed by the laws of war. That meant I wanted it dropped on a military target."

B **From 'The Roots of European Security' by Vadim Nekrasov, 1984.**

"The Americans dropped atom bombs on the Japanese cities of Hiroshima and Nagasaki on August 6 and 9, killing hundreds of thousands of civilians. Officially Washington 'claimed that' the bombings were aimed at bringing the end of the war nearer and avoiding unnecessary bloodshed and casualties. But they had entirely different objectives. Neither strategy nor tactics required the use of the atom bomb. Indeed the proposal to end the war made after the bombings was right away rejected by the military leaders of Japan. The purpose of the bombings was to intimidate other countries, above all the Soviet Union. In other words the US decision to use atomic energy for military purposes was meant to produce a diplomatic and psychological impact, and this has since involved the world in a nuclear arms race."

C **From 'Sanity, the Voice of CND', August 1985.**

"The Japanese were on the verge of surrender. In mid-July they sent out peace feelers via Sato, the Japanese ambassadors in Moscow. The Soviet Union blocked the proposals because, according to the Yalta agreement, they were due to enter the war against Japan three months after VE day, and they were ready and keen to do so in early August.

General Groves, the engineer director of the Manhatten project, was desperate to see the fruits of his – and the project's – labours before the end of war. The military equipment was available and had been developed at a cost of $2,000 million. It would have been difficult to justify not using it after such a vast financial investment.

Truman was very impressed with what he heard and believed, along with most of his advisers, that if the bomb could be built it should be used. For some reason the scientists failed to mention the long term dangers of radiation.

Both bombs were atomic bombs. The Nagasaki bomb produced a greater blast. Some of the leaders of the Manhattan project were keen for both types of bomb to be tested. Nagasaki was, in short, an experiment."

D British cartoon, 1960.

'Don't you see, they had to find out if it worked . . .'

Document questions

1 *Compare Documents* **A** *and* **B**.
   a Write a sentence to describe one important difference in the way Documents **A** and **B** explain why the atom bomb was dropped. Support your answer with a quotation from Document **A** and a quotation from Document **B**.
   b Why do you think Documents **A** and **B** give such different versions of the reasons for the dropping of the bomb? Give two reasons.
   c What are 'memoirs'? (Document **A**). Suggest a reason why memoirs might be seen as an unreliable or unhelpful source of historical evidence.

2 **a** How might the author of Document **C** have reacted to Truman's claim in Document **A** that he had asked the committee 'to study with great care the implications the new weapon might have for us'? Explain your answer and support it with a quotation from Document **C**.
   b Why might Document **C** be seen as a biased source of historical evidence about the bombing of Hiroshima?
   c If Document **C** is biased, does that mean it is no use to the historian? Explain your answer.

3 Do you think the person who drew Document **D** would have agreed more with the explanation given by Truman in Document **A** for the dropping of the atomic bomb, or with the explanation given in Document **C**? Support your answer with quotations from at least two documents.

Follow-on questions

4 How do you think the person who drew Document **D** would have reacted to Truman's statement in Document **A** that 'I wanted to make sure that it (the bomb) would be used in a manner prescribed by the laws of war'? Explain your answer carefully.

5 In what way might the bombing of Hiroshima have led to a worsening of the 'cold war'? Explain your answer and support it with a quotation from one of the documents.

7.1 Long march

A **Mao's four slogans of red army guerilla tactics, 1937.**

"When the enemy advances, we retreat
When he camps, we harass
When he tires, we attack
When he retreats, we pursue"

B **The red army's code of conduct, 1928.**
Replace all doors when you leave a house.
Return and roll up the straw matting on which you slept.
Be courteous and polite to the people and help them when you can.
Return all borrowed articles.
Replace all damaged articles.
Be honest in transactions with the peasants.
Pay for all articles purchased.
Be sanitary, and especially establish latrines a safe distance from people's houses.

C **'The Red Army Marching to Victory' – official communist party poster, after 1949.**

D **From 'The Long March' by Robert Goldston, 1971.**
"Red army units spent more time helping peasants work their fields, setting up village schools and hospitals, and ceaselessly propagandizing, than they did in fighting. Peasants were never drafted into the red army – they were encouraged to volunteer. Peasant supplies and belongings were never seized by the red army – they were bought and paid for. And within red army controlled areas, land was distributed to the landless. Landlords were expelled and control of village affairs was entrusted directly to the people of the village. These people could see for themselves that the red army lived no better than they did; furthermore the Chinese communist leaders, from Mao Tse-tung down shared all the trials and hardships of the common soldier."

Document questions

1 Copy out two of the four slogans quoted in Document [A] and write a sentence to explain what you think the idea behind these slogans was and why the red army used these tactics.

2 *Compare Documents* [B] *and* [D]. Does the red army seem to have obeyed the rules of the code of conduct? Write 'yes' or 'no'. Support your answer with two examples from Document [D] and two rules from Document [B].

3 a Give a reason suggested in Document [C] that explains why the red army was able to 'march to victory'. Remember to describe what you see in the poster in your answer.
  b Suggest one reason why Document [C] might be seen as a biased source of historical evidence.

4 Write a paragraph to explain why you think Mao Tse-tung was a successful leader. Back up your answer with evidence from the documents.

Follow-on questions

5 What was the long march (Document [D])? Write a paragraph to explain why it took place and what happened.

6 Write a report to Mao's enemy in the civil war, Chiang Kai-shek, written by the commander of troops sent on an unsuccessful mission to locate red army guerillas. Explain why the red army is so hard to beat and suggest what will need to be done to beat them.

7.2 The great leap forward

A Chinese propaganda painting showing the hopes of the great leap forward.

B Statements by Mao Tse-tung.
"During a tour of the country made in 1958 I witnessed the tremendous energy of the people. On this foundation it is possible to succeed at any task whatsoever . . . It is better to set up People's Communes. Their advantage lies in the fact that they combine industry, agriculture, commerce, education and military affairs . . . After a number of years, Chinese society will enter into the age of communism, where the principles from each according to his ability, to each according to his needs will be practised."

C From 'Eyewitness in China' by Hugo Portisch (a journalist visiting China at the time of the great leap forward).
"There were not enough machines, there was no cement, no mortar and other building materials. Pekingers were summoned to build this dam with their bare hands and feet by voluntary shift work. Hundreds of thousands of inhabitants of Peking, including all the civil servants and university professors, doctors, students, etc. set out to execute the order. In eight-hour shifts they worked day and night without a break. They scratched away the earth from the surrounding hills often with no more than their finger nails, they split stones with the most primitive tools, and carried earth and stone in little baskets on carrying-poles to the river bed, where more thousands stood and stamped the stones and earth flat with their feet, urged on by the party cadre men with megaphones. They shouted slogans, urged the masses on, ordered them to work harder and faster. Mao Tse-tung himself and all the members of the Politburo and the government came and joined in the work of building the dam. In six months the dam was built. It is 2,088 feet high and 38.2 feet wide at its base."

D Soviet criticisms of the great leap forward quoted in 'The True Face of Maoism' by Burlatsky, 1969.

"We could not help feeling doubts about the plan to increase steel output in the People's Republic of China from 5 million to 80–100 million tons in five years, and to increase total industrial output six and a half times over. These targets were not based on any sensible economic calculations. We could not fail to feel alarmed when, with every step they took, the leaders of the People's Republic of China began to pour abuse on Lenin's idea that mankind can pass directly only to socialism, which must inevitably evolve gradually into communism. They also abandoned Lenin's idea of paying workers and went over instead to the egalitarian distribution in the people's communes."

Document questions

1 **a** Name the Chinese communist leader shown on the flag in Document **A**.
   b Why do you think the people in the painting are shown on horseback?
   c Besides the flag, what are the people carrying in their hands? Why are they shown carrying these things?
   d Document **A** is a propaganda painting. Does that mean it is useless to the historian of the great leap forward? Explain your answer carefully.

2 According to Document **B**, what did Mao hope would be the eventual result or benefit for China of the great leap forward?

3 **a** Do Documents **B** and **C** agree or disagree about the enthusiasm of the Chinese people? Explain your answer and support it with a quotation from each of the two documents.
   b What clues are there in Documents **C** and **D** as to why the great leap forward failed? Explain your answer and include a quotation from each of the two documents.

4 Why is Document **D** so critical of the great leap forward? Give reasons for your answer and quote from Document **D**.

5 How useful to the historian of the great leap forward is the evidence of foreign journalists (as in Document **C**)?

Follow-on questions

6 What was the difference between 'communes' (Document **D**) and Soviet collective farms?

7 What political changes were brought about in China after the failure of the great leap forward?

7.3 The cultural revolution

A Photograph of a demonstration in China, October 1966.

B From *Peking Review*, October 18 1966.
"The sky was azure and Peking basked in the golden sunshine (when) the great mass of red guards and revolutionary teachers and students, militant and alert and with red flags and portraits of Chairman Mao held high, began converging from all directions on the T'ien An Men Square . . . These young fighters . . . each carrying a copy of the bright red-covered 'Quotations From Chairman Mao' . . . formed a magnificent stream of red. They recited over and over again passages from Chairman Mao's writing. At ten minutes to one the majestic strains of 'The East Is Red' were struck up . . . Countless hands waved dazzling copies of 'Quotations From Chairman Mao' and countless pairs of eyes turned toward the direction of the reddest red sun . . . When Chairman Mao drove past the ranks . . . many students quickly opened their copies of 'Quotations From Chairman Mao' and wrote the same words on the fly leaf. 'At 1.10 p.m. on October 18, the most, most happy and the most, most unforgettable moment in my life, I saw Chairman Mao, the never-setting red sun!'"

C Photograph of a wall poster in China, 1966.

Document questions

1 a Name the book held by the young people in Document **A**.
  b Is the photograph a primary or a secondary source? Explain your answer.
  c What do you think was the political reason why all the people in the photograph wore very similar clothes?
  d By what political name were the young people shown in the photograph known at the time of the cultural revolution?

2 a Document **B** could be called a 'biased' source of evidence – explain why and support your answer with a quotation from the document.
  b Just because Document **B** may be biased, does that mean it is useless to the historian of the cultural revolution as evidence? Explain your answer.

3 What do you think was the aim or purpose of the poster shown in Document **C**? Support your answer by mentioning things in the poster.

4 Name two pieces of evidence from the documents which suggest that Mao's form of communism was like a religion. Explain your answer.

Follow-on questions

5 In which city did the demonstration shown in Document **A** take place?

6 How and why did the cultural revolution end?

7 *Compare these documents with those on the cult of personality (page 64).* What important similarities and differences do you notice in the way in which the leader is shown?

7.4 China meets America

A Photograph of a meeting in Peking between two leaders, February 1972.

B Statement from Richard M. Nixon in the Kennedy–Nixon TV debates, 1960.
"What do the Chinese Communists want? They don't want just Quemoy and Matsu; they don't want just Formosa; they want the world. And the question is if you surrender or indicate in advance that you're not going to defend any part of the free world, and you figure that's going to satisfy them, it doesn't satisfy them. It only whets their appetite; and then the question comes, when do you stop them?"

C Richard M. Nixon in 'Asia after Vietnam', 1967.
"Any American policy towards Asia must come urgently to grips with the reality of China. This does not mean, as many would simplistically have it, rushing to grant recognition to Peking, to admit it to the United Nations and to ply it with offers of trade – all of which would serve to confirm its rulers in their present course. It does mean recognizing the present and potential danger from communist China, and taking measures designed to meet the danger.

Ten years from now the communist Chinese, for example, among others, may have a significant nuclear capability. They will not be a major nuclear power, but they will have a significant nuclear capability. By that time the war in Vietnam will be over . . . and we are going to try to make the break-through in some normalization of our relations with Communist China."

D From *The Times of India*, February 29 1972.

"It all began at least ten years ago with the Sino–Soviet split . . . the more discerning Americans began to recognise that China did not constitute a threat to their vital interests. But two additional developments had to take place before an American president could think in terms of visiting Peking . . . As a result of the US failure to win the extremely cruel and senseless war in Indochina, despite a colossal investment in men and resources, the American people have lost the will and the desire to serve as the world's policeman. They have recognised that their power to impose their will on the rest of the world is not unlimited. Simultaneously, through two purges – one at the time of the cultural revolution and the other last summer – Chairman Mao Tse-tung has got rid of colleagues who were ready to make common cause with the Soviet Union against the United States."

Document questions

1 a Name the two political leaders seen in Document **A**.
   b From what you know about their political ideas, write a couple of sentences to explain why it was unusual or strange that the two leaders shown in the photograph should meet.

2 a Describe one way in which Documents **B** and **C** show different attitudes towards China. Support your explanation with quotations from the documents.
   b Why is it a little surprising that Documents **B** and **C** contain very different attitudes towards China?

3 *Compare Documents* **C** *and* **D**. Why do you think Documents **C** and **D** give such different views of the importance of the Vietnam war?

4 What doubts might a historian have in trusting TV debates between politicians (as in Document **B**) as historical evidence? Give reasons for your answer.

5 *Look at Document* **A** *and read the other documents.* Explain why it might be useful for the 'image' of the man on the right hand side of the photograph to have this published.

Follow-on questions

6 *Read Document* **B**. Who was 'Kennedy' and what, besides China, were the TV debates about?

7 Where is 'Formosa' (Document **B**), and why would the Chinese communists want it?

8 When was 'Peking' admitted to the United Nations and whose place did it take?

8.1   The Suez crisis

A **Part of a letter from President Eisenhower to Prime Minister Anthony Eden.**

"I urge you to avoid the use of force, at least until it has been proved to the world that the United Nations is incapable of handling the problem. To invade Egypt merely because that country has chosen to nationalise a company, will be seen by the world as power politics and raise a storm of resentment."

B **Draft resolution proposed to the UN Security Council by the USA, October 30 1956.**

"Noting that the armed forces of Israel have penetrated deeply into Egyptian territory in violation of the general armistice agreement between Egypt and Israel.

a Calls upon Israel immediately to withdraw its armed forces.

b Calls upon all members to refrain from the use of force and not to give military or financial help to Israel until it complies with this resolution."

C **Resolution to the UN General Assembly by the USA, November 1 1956.**

"Noting that the armed forces of France and the UK are conducting military operations against Egypt and that traffic through the Suez Canal is now interrupted.

a Urges that all parties now involved in hostilities agree to an immediate ceasefire.

b Withdraw all forces behind the armistice lines and keep the armistice agreements."

D **From *Davar* (Israeli newspaper), November 2 1956.**

"The League of Nations failed when the world was threatened with the danger of Nazism, and up to now the UN has failed before the threat of Nasserish dictatorship. The UN was incapable of ensuring the implementation of the armistice agreements and was too weak to prevent the provocations by Arab aggression against Israel. The efforts made in the UN for a peaceful settlement of the Suez dispute in accordance with international law also failed."

E **From *Pravda* (Soviet newspaper), November 2 1956.**

"HANDS OFF EGYPT

In defiance of the UN charter and the principles of international law, the Anglo–French imperialists have launched an intervention against the independent Egyptian Republic in an attempt to seize by armed force the Suez Canal.

While the English and French diplomats were paralyzing the security council and preventing it from taking the necessary measures to stop Israeli aggression, the armed forces of England and France began intervention against Egypt. Responsibility for the solution of this problem falls now upon the extraordinary session of the general assembly of the UN, called by the decision of the majority of the security council members."

Document questions

1 a *Read Documents* A *and* C. What evidence is there that the United Kingdom did not obey the American president's request? Quote from both documents in your answer.

  b Suggest a reason why it might seem surprising that the American president's request should not be obeyed.

2 *Compare Documents* B *and* D.

  a How would you describe the attitude of the Israelis towards the UN?

  b How does Document D help explain or understand the Israeli attitude?

Support each answer with a quotation.

3 Write a sentence to explain one way in which Documents C and E show similar attitudes towards what was happening in Egypt. Include a quotation from both documents.

4 Explain carefully why it is perhaps surprising that Documents C and E should agree at all (think of who wrote the documents).

5 Explain two ways in which the British government did badly out of the Suez crisis. Support each explanation with a quotation from the documents.

Follow-on questions

6 a Name the company that Egypt had chosen to nationalise (Document A).

  b Suggest a reason why many countries were particularly interested in what happened to this company.

7 Document E mentions the UN charter. How had it been broken in the Suez crisis?

8 Carefully explain one way in which the Suez crisis could be called a success for the UN, and one way in which it seemed to be a failure for the UN. Give a quotation each time.

8.2   The six day war

A Maps showing Middle-East borders before and after the six day war, 1967.

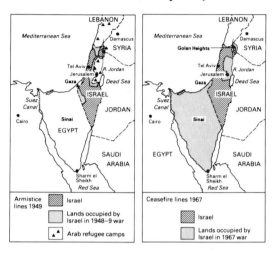

C Statement by Gamel Abdel Nasser at a press conference in Cairo, May 28 1967.
"We accept no kind of co-existence with Israel. The rights of Palestinians should be given back to them. What happened in 1948 was an aggression against the people of Palestine. Israel expelled the Palestinians from their country and stole their property. Nevertheless we see that the USA and some major powers like Britain say they are protecting Israel. We, the Arabs, are an ancient people with an ancient civilization going back 7,000 years. We can wait and we do not forget easily. When the crusaders occupied our country we were under their rule for 70 years, but finally they were gone and only their castles remained behind as historical ruins. Therefore, no Arab will ever give up the rights of the Palestinian people."

B 'The line-up of forces' – adapted from surveys published in *The Guardian*, May 19 and 24 1967.

ISRAEL		EGYPT	
Regular Forces	17,000	Regular Forces	190,000
Reservists	204,000	Reservists	120,000
Tanks and armour	1,050	Tanks and Armour	1,200
Aircraft and American 'Hawk' Missiles	350	Aircraft and Russian Missiles	550
		JORDAN	
		Forces	65,000
		Tanks	132
		Aircraft	12
		SYRIA	
		Forces	81,000
		Tanks	350
		Aircraft	102
		IRAQ	
		Forces	82,000
		Tanks	320
		Aircraft	87
		LEBANON	
		Forces	11,000
		Aircraft	8

D Speech in the House of Lords by Lord Sieff, president of Marks and Spencer.
"We may sit comfortably in London and contemplate the threat of annihilation because it is something which is at a distance, but the people who live in Israel are genuinely afraid of being swept off the face of the earth, as the Arab leaders have said so frequently. I have relatives there, and I know their fears and how they regard this danger which confronts them. The people of Israel appear to me to be exceedingly brave. I can think of no case of a sovereign state such as Israel being eliminated by the threat of brute force exercised by its neighbours. This is not a moment when the people who have to bear the brunt of threat and attack will be pleased to discuss with us the niceties of international law."

E Casualty figures for the 1967 war.

Israeli	Egyptian front	Jordanian front	Syrian front	Total
Killed	275	299	115	689
Wounded	800	1,457	306	2,563
Arab (*estimates*)				
Killed	10,000	1,000	2,500	13,500
Wounded	20,000	2,000	5,000	27,000

Document questions

1 *Look at Document* **A** *(i) and Document* **B**. Give two reasons why it would be difficult for Israel to win a war against the Arabs.

2 a Suggest two reasons why the figures in Document **B** might give a misleading or unreliable impression of the military strength of the Israelis and the Arabs.
b What evidence is there in the table that the six day war was not just an Arab–Israeli war, but a clash between the super powers?

3 *Read Document* **C**. How does it help explain why a war might break out at some time between the Arabs and the Israelis? Explain your answer and back it up with a quotation from the Document.

4 *Read Document* **D**. How does it help explain why the Israeli army might do well in a war against the Arabs? Explain your answer and back it up with a quotation from the document.

5 What are the advantages and disadvantages to the historian of the six day war of using casualty figures (as in Document **E**) as evidence?

6 Using the evidence in the documents, write a paragraph to explain how successful you think the six day war of 1967 was for the Israelis. Mention things from the documents which you think help answer this question.

Follow-on questions

7 a Who was Nasser (Document **C**)?
b How successful was the six day war for Nasser?

8 In Document **C** Nasser refers to the events of 1948. Write a few sentences to describe what happened in 1948 – to what events was he referring?

9 Give three reasons suggested in the documents to help explain why the Arab–Israeli conflict was so difficult to solve. Support each reason with a quotation from the documents.

8.3 Dawson's Field hijack

A **A summary of newspaper reports, September 26, October 3, 1970.**
"In an act of air piracy unique in the history of aviation, three civilian airliners – two American and one Swiss – were hijacked within a few hours of each other on September 6 by Arab commandos of the Popular Front for the Liberation of Palestine (PFLP), the left wing guerilla organisation. Two of the airliners were flown to a desert airstrip called Dawson's Field in Jordan where passengers and crew were held by PFLP guerillas; the third was flown to Cairo where it was blown up minutes after the passengers and crew had left the aircraft. On the same day the PFLP made an unsuccessful attempt to hijack an Israeli airliner over the coast of England. An Arab woman, Leila Khaled, was taken into custody after the plane had made an emergency landing at Heathrow. Three days later, a British airliner was hijacked by the PFLP and flown to the same desert airfield at Dawson's Field where the American and Swiss planes had been taken to."

B **Adapted from a statement by guerillas of the Popular Front for the Liberation of Palestine, September 6 1970.**
"This action is aimed against the Middle-East peace talks. It is also a blow against the American plot to liquidate the Palestinian cause by supplying arms to Israel. The Swiss airliner and its passengers will be held until the Swiss government releases the three Arabs serving long term prison sentences in Swiss jails for the attack on an Israeli airliner at Zurich airport."

C **Statement by United Nations Secretary General, U. Thant, September 8 1970.**
"These criminal acts of hijacking planes, of detaining passengers and crew, of blowing up aircraft, and of the detention of passengers in transit, are most deplorable and must be condemned. It is high time that the international community through the appropriate agencies and organizations, adopted prompt and effective measures to put a stop to this return to the law of the jungle."

D **Statement by Leila Khaled, Palestinian Arab and PFLP hijacker.**
"I do not see how my oppressor could sit in judgement on my response to his oppressive actions against me. He is in no position to render an impartial judgement or accuse me of air piracy and hijacking when he has hijacked me and my people out of our land. My deed cannot be judged without examining the underlying causes."

E **Photograph of the blowing up of the hijacked planes at Dawson's Field, Jordan, September 1970.**

F Statement from 10 Downing Street, October 1 1970.

"On September 12 the British government stated that they were prepared to release Miss Leila Khaled as part of a satisfactory solution of the problem of the hostages from the three hijacked aircraft. As a result of negotiations in which both the Red Cross and the government of the UAR have taken part, all the hostages have now reached safety.

The British government has arranged with the governments of the Federal German Republic and Switzerland for Miss Khaled together with six Palestinian Arabs in the custody of the German and Swiss authorities to be flown out."

Document questions

1 *Read Document A.*
  a What is a 'guerilla organisation'?
  b What evidence is there that Document A was biased against the PFLP?

2 *Read Document B.* Why do you think the PFLP chose a Swiss airliner to hijack?

3 **a** What do you think U. Thant meant in Document C by 'this return to the law of the jungle'?
  b Why are the attitudes towards hijacking expressed in Document C so different from those mentioned in Documents A and D?
  c How useful to the historian of the Dawson's Field hijack do you think is Leila Khaled's statement (Document D) as evidence?

4 What does Document E show, and why do you think the PFLP was keen for it to be published?

5 *Read Document F and look again at the other documents.* Write a paragraph to explain whether you think the hijack was a success or a failure for the PFLP. You don't have to quote.

6 Write a few sentences to explain ways in which the PFLP could be seen as
  a terrorists (write what the hijackers' opponents would say about them), and
  b freedom fighters (write what the hijackers' supporters would say about them).

Follow-on questions

7 'Peace talks' (Document B) seem like a good idea – so why were the PFLP opposed to them? Give reasons.

8 *Look at Document F.* How did government ideas about the way to deal with terrorism change in the years that followed this hijack?

9 Write a letter to a newspaper in which you criticise the action taken by Mr Heath (Document F). Give reasons for your criticisms and suggest alternative ways of dealing with hijackers. Give reasons for your suggestions.

8.4   Camp David

A Statement by US President Carter at Camp David, USA, March 26 1979.
"We have won at last the first step of peace, a first step on a long and difficult road. We must rededicate ourselves to the goal of a broader peace with justice for all who have lived in a state of conflict in the Middle-East. I am convinced that other Arab people need and want peace. But some of their leaders are not yet willing to honour these needs and desires for peace. We must now demonstrate the advantages of peace and expand its benefits to encompass all those who have suffered so much in the Middle-East."

B From *Palestine*, the PLO information bulletin, September 1980.
"All the faked talks (without the Palestinians) on Palestinian 'self rule' will lead nowhere and the entire Camp David process will not bring the region closer to a comprehensive peace. In reality the US does not want peace in the area as long as a major military outbreak is avoided. On the contrary, American imperialist circles try to provoke continuous tension as much as possible. They prop up their own military bases and those of their clients in Israel, Egypt and elsewhere. They try to pressure their clients into handing over more oil and more money to the US. Israel continues to be armed to the teeth."

C Statement by Egyptian President Sadat at Camp David, USA, March 26 1979.
"President Carter once said that the United States is committed without reservation to seeing the peace process through until all parties to the Arab—Israeli conflict are at peace. We value such a promise from a leader who raised the banners of morality as a substitute for power politics and opportunism. The liberation of Arab land and the reinstitution of Arab authority in the West Bank and Gaza would certainly enhance our common strategic interests."

D Statement by Israeli Prime Minister Menachem Begin at Camp David, USA, March 26 1979.
"The signature is the third greatest day of my life. The first was May 14 1948 when our flag was hoisted and our independence in our ancestors' land proclaimed after 1878 years of dispersion, persecution, humiliation and, ultimately, physical destruction. The second day was when Jerusalem became one city and our brave soldiers embraced with tears and kissed the ancient stones of the wall destined to protect the chosen place of God's glory."

Document questions

1 Which two Middle-Eastern countries made peace with each other at Camp David?

2 Do Documents A and B agree or disagree about whether the Camp David talks had brought peace any nearer in the Middle-East? Write a sentence to explain your answers and quote from both documents.

3 Write a sentence to explain one important difference between the attitudes towards American policy in the Middle-East as shown in Documents B and C. Support your explanation with quotations from both documents.

4 a Why do you think the ideas in Documents B and C are so different? Explain your answer.
   b What are the advantages and disadvantages to the historian of Camp David of using the PLO information bulletin (Document B) as evidence?

5 What important difference do you notice in Documents C and D between Egyptian and Israeli attitudes towards the land?
   Write a sentence to explain your answer and support it with a quotation from Document C and one from Document D.

6 Suggest two important reasons why the rest of the Arab world was so unwilling to join in with the Camp David peace process. Support your explanation with two quotations from the documents.

Follow-on questions

7 Write paragraphs to explain in your own words the most important advantages and disadvantages of the Camp David agreement for:
   a President Sadat, and
   b Menachem Begin.
   Explain your answers as carefully as you can and remember to describe the advantages and disadvantages for each man.

8 Why were the 'West Bank and Gaza' of such 'strategic interest' to Israel? (Document C).

9.1   McCarthyism

A Statements made by Senator Joseph McCarthy to the Senate inquiry into communist penetration of the State Department, March 8 1950.
"Professor Owen Lattimore has been a 'pro-communist' for many years. He is the architect of our Far-Eastern policy and is the leading member of a group which has delivered China to communism and has done everything in the Far East that Russia wants. He is the top Russian espionage agent."

(McCarthy was a leading figure in the 'Committee for Un-American Activities', referred to in Document D.)

B Statement on April 6 1950 by Professor Owen Lattimore to the same inquiry mentioned in Document A.
"I have never been a communist or a sympathiser with communism. I have never held a position in the US government in which I could make policy. Far from accepting communist policy on China I vigorously supported Chiang Kai-shek when the communists were attacking him. By telling the kind of lies about the USA that Russian propagandists couldn't invent, Senator McCarthy is accomplishing results for Russia which exceed their wildest hopes. I accuse Senator McCarthy of making the US government an object of suspicion in the eyes of the anti-communist world and, undoubtedly, the laughing stock of the communist governments. He has surrounded himself with crackpots, professional informers and hysterics."

C Speech by US President Harry Truman, Washington, April 24 1950.
"The Federal Employee Loyalty Program was set up to ensure that no disloyal person, whether a communist or a member of the Ku Klux Klan should be employed by the government and that loyal employees should be protected against false, malicious and ill-founded accusations. The government is fighting communism without headlines or hysteria, but does not intend to turn the FBI into a Gestapo, or to try to control what our people read and say and think, or to turn the USA into a right wing totalitarian country."

D British cartoon, 1948.

Document questions

1 Quote two accusations made by Senator McCarthy about Professor Lattimore in Document [A].

2 a Quote two pieces of evidence given by Professor Lattimore in Document [B] to deny Senator McCarthy's accusations.

  b Write a couple of sentences to explain what you think Professor Lattimore meant when he said in Document [B]: 'By telling the kind of lies about the USA that Russian propagandists couldn't invent, Senator McCarthy is accomplishing results for Russia which exceed their wildest hopes'.

  c Who was 'Chiang Kai-shek' (Document [B])?

3 a Write a couple of sentences in your own words to explain why you think President Truman set up the federal employee loyalty program. You don't need to quote.

  b Do you think President Truman would have approved or disapproved of Joe McCarthy's methods of fighting communism? Explain your answer and support it with quotations from Documents [B] and [C].

4 Do you think the person who drew Document [D] was a supporter or a critic of McCarthy's committee for un-American activities? Explain your answer and support it by mentioning at least four things in the cartoon.

Follow-on questions

5 Who were the 'Gestapo' (Document [C])?

6 Who else besides professors and politicians were brought before Senator McCarthy's committee for un-American activities?

7 In what way was McCarthyism a part of the cold war?

8 How did the 'McCarthyite' period end?

9.2   Civil rights

A **Photograph of a civil rights march in Washington, USA, 1963.**

B **Statement by Desmond Tutu, Bishop of Johannesburg, on the TV documentary programme, 'Witness to Apartheid', 1986.**
"People are fond of drawing parallels between what is happening in our country and what happened in the sixties in the United States, with the civil rights movement, and to some extent there are similarities. But there is one fundamental difference. The law in the United States was on the side of those who were campaigning in the civil rights movement. What Martin Luther King and those involved with him were doing was to claim rights that were theirs under the constitution of the law. The constitution and the law are against us, so we have to overturn and dismantle that whole structure. In South Africa it is not a question of civil rights. It is a question really of fundamental human rights, the recognition that a black person is a human being created in the image of God. The situation in South Africa is violent, and the primary violence in this land is the violence of apartheid."

C **From an American supreme court ruling, 1954.**
"We have this day held that the equal protection clause of the fourteenth amendment to the constitution forbids the States from maintaining racially segregated public schools. . . . Segregation in public education denies negro children their freedom. We hold that racial segregation breaks the law guaranteed by the constitution."

D **From the 'Kerner Report', an inquiry into the race riots in American cities in 1967.**
"About two-thirds of the lowest income group – or 20 per cent of all negroes – are making no significant economic gains despite continued general prosperity. Half of these 'hard-core disadvantaged' – more than two million persons – live in central city neighborhoods. Recent special censuses in Los Angeles and Cleveland indicate that the incomes of persons living in the worst slum areas have not risen at all during this period, unemployment rates have declined only slightly; the proportion of families with female heads has increased, and housing conditions have worsened even though rents have risen. One third of all unemployed negroes in 1967 were the 16–19 year olds. 53% of the rioters arrested were under 25. Two-thirds of rioters interviewed believed it impossible to get the job they wanted."

Document questions

1 *Look at Document* A.
  a Name two of the 'civil rights' that the protestors are demanding.
  b What type of protest is seen in the photograph? Why was this type of protest often used – what was the advantage of it?
  c How useful are photographs (as in Document A) to the historian of civil rights as evidence?

2 *Read Document* B. What difference does Bishop Tutu notice in the problems of race relations between South Africa and the USA?

3 How can the supreme court ruling (Document C) be used to support Bishop Tutu's comments about the differences in the problems of race relations between South Africa and the USA? Support your answer with a quotation from Document C.

4 How far, according to the Kerner report (Document D) had the demands of the civil rights protestors shown in Document A been met? Support your answer with quotations from the documents.

5 How useful to the historian of race relations are TV interviews (as in Document B) as evidence?

Follow-on questions

6 Compare these documents with those on apartheid (page 114). What similarities do you notice in the problems of race relations between South Africa and the USA? Quote evidence from the documents.

7 Compare these documents with those on Martin Luther King (page 106). Explain why you think many negro Americans turned away from King's methods and used violence? Quote evidence from the documents to support your answer.

9.3 Martin Luther King

A The idea of 'Satyagraha' (non-resistance) described by Mohandas K. Gandhi, the Indian civil rights leader.
"Soul force, or the power of truth, is reached by the infliction of suffering, not on your opponent, but on yourself. Rivers of blood may have to flow before we gain our freedom, but it must be our blood . . . The government of the day had passed a law which I do not like. If by using violence I force the government to change the law, I am using what may be called body-force. If I do not obey the law, and accept the penalty for breaking it, I use soul force. It involves sacrificing yourself."

B American negro civil rights leader Martin Luther King reacts to the bombing of his house in Montgomery, Alabama, January 30 1955.
"While King was speaking at a meeting a bomb was thrown into his home. There was smoke everywhere. When King arrived, the house was ringed by an angry negro crowd armed with guns, rocks, rods, knives, sticks and bottles. It was clear that Montgomery was on the verge of a bloodbath.

King raised his arms: 'Don't do anything panicky at all. Don't get your weapons. He who lives by the sword will die by the sword. We are not advocating violence. I want you to love our enemies, and let them know you love them. I want it to be known across the land that if I am stopped, this movement will not stop and our work will not stop, for what we are doing is right'. As King finished, cries of 'God bless you' came from the crowd, which began to leave.

This moment changed the course of the protest and made King a living symbol. He, and other members of the boycott committee, had spoken of love and forgiveness. But now, seeing the idea in action, millions were touched, if not converted. The 'parable of the porch' went out over the newsmedia and King's name became a token to almost all American negroes."

C Photograph of Martin Luther King in Baltimore, 1964.

D Photograph of Martin Luther King on the steps of the Lincoln Memorial, 1957.

Document questions

1 *Read Document* **A**. What do you think Gandhi meant by 'soul force' and why might it be hard to achieve? Support your answer with a quotation from Document **A**.

2 What evidence is there in Document **B** that Martin Luther King was following Gandhi's idea of soul force?

3 Suggest reasons why Martin Luther King would not use violence. Support your answer with a quotation from Document **B**.

4 What do Documents **C** and **D** show, and how do you think photographs like these helped win support for Martin Luther King?

5 What do you think we learn about Martin Luther King's personality from these documents – what sort of a person was he? Support your answer with quotations from the documents.

6 Document **B** is from a biography of Martin Luther King, published in 1966, two years before he died. What are the advantages and disadvantages to the historian of race relations of using this source as evidence?

Follow-on questions

7 Document **B** mentions the 'boycott' at Montgomery. How did it start and why was it successful?

8 *Compare these documents with the evidence about Gandhi's salt protest (page 110).* What similarities do you notice in the ideas and behaviour of the demonstrators? What similarities do you notice in the methods used by the authorities to stop the demonstrations?

9.4 Vietnam – media war

[A] Statement by BBC commentator Robin Day to a seminar of the Royal United Service Institution.

"The war on colour television screens in American living rooms has made Americans far more anti-militarist and anti-war than anything else. One wonders if in future a democracy which has uninhibited television coverage in every home will ever be able to fight a war, however just. The full brutality of the combat will be there in close-up and in colour, and blood looks very red on the colour television screen."

[B] Extract from a *Newsweek* survey on opinions of the Vietnam war, 1967.

"Television seems to have encouraged a majority of viewers to support the war. 64 per cent said television had made them 'feel like backing up the boys in Vietnam'. 26 per cent felt moved to oppose the war."

[C] Extract from 'Kurt Volkert – Combat Cameraman Vietnam', 1968.

"A cameraman feels so inadequate, being able to record only a minute part of the misery, a minute part of the fighting. You have to decide what the most important action is. Is it the woman holding her crying baby? Is it the young girl cringing near her house because of the exploding grenades? Or is it the defiant looking Vietcong with blood on his face just after capture?"

[D] Article by war reporter Richard Lindley in the *Spectator*, July 1 1972.

"What television *really* wanted was action in which the men died cleanly and not too bloodily. When they get a film which shows what a mortar does to a man, really shows the flesh torn and the blood flowing, they get squeamish. They want it to be just so. They want television to be cinema."

[E] Photograph of the execution of a Vietcong suspect.

Document questions

1 a What difference do you notice between the opinions quoted in Documents A and B about the effect TV had on public opinion about the Vietnam war? Quote from both documents in your answer.

b What doubts might the historian of the Vietnam war have in using opinion polls (as in Document B) as evidence?

2 What do you think Robin Day meant when he said in Document A 'One wonders if in future a democracy which has uninhibited television coverage in every home will ever be able to fight a war, however just'?

3 Document E has been described as one of the most famous images of the Vietnam war. What was it about this photograph which made such an impact on people? Support your answer by mentioning things in the photograph.

4 What do you think Richard Lindley meant when he said in Document D 'They want television to be cinema'?

5 *Look at the documents again.* Then
a suggest two reasons why the US government decided not to cut down the amount of TV coverage of the war, and
b explain what are the advantages and disadvantages to the historian of the Vietnam war of using TV as evidence.

Follow-on questions

6 How did TV help make Vietnam very different from all previous wars?

7 From what you have read and seen in these documents, do you think TV had anything to do with America's losing the Vietnam war? Give reasons for your answer.

8 In what ways did people in the USA show their opposition to the Vietnam war?

10.1 Gandhi's salt protest

A Part of a letter from Mahatma Gandhi to Lord Irwin, British Viceroy of India, March 2 1930.

"And why do I regard the British rule as a curse?

It has made poor the millions by a system of exploitation and by a ruinous expensive military and civil government which the country can never afford.

It has reduced us politically to slavery. The British system seems designed to crush the very life out of the peasant. Even the salt he must use to live is so taxed as to make the burden fall heaviest on him.

My ambition is: to convert the British people through non-violence, and thus make them see the wrong they have done to India. If the Indian people join me, the sufferings they will undergo will be enough to melt the stoniest hearts. This non-violence will be expressed through civil disobedience.

If my letter makes no appeal to your heart, I shall proceed to disregard the salt laws. It is, I know, open to you to arrest me, I hope that there will be tens of thousands ready to take up the work after me.

This letter is not in any way intended as a threat but is a simple and sacred duty on a civil resister. Your sincere friend,
M. K. Gandhi."

B Newspaper report by the American journalist Webb Miller, describing a march by 2,500 of Gandhi's followers to the Dharsana salt works, May 21 1930.

"When a picked group of the marchers approached, police officers ordered them to retreat. They continued to advance. Suddenly at a word of command, scores of native policemen rushed upon the advancing marchers and rained blows on their heads with their steel-shod lathis★. Not one of the marchers even raised an arm to fend off the blows. They went down like nine-pins. Those struck down fell sprawling, unconscious, or writhing with fractured skulls or broken shoulders. The survivors silently and doggedly marched on until struck down.

In 18 years of reporting in 22 countries, I never witnessed such harrowing scenes as at Dharsana. One surprising feature was the discipline of volunteers. It seemed they were thoroughly imbued with Gandhi's non-violent creed."

★ *clubs*

C From a letter from Lord Irwin to King George V, May 22 1930.

"Your Majesty can hardly fail to have read with amusement the accounts of the several battles for the salt depot. Most of the casualties were shamming."

A FRANKENSTEIN OF THE EAST.
Gandhi. "REMEMBER—NO VIOLENCE; JUST DISOBEDIENCE."
Genie. "AND WHAT IF I DISOBEY *YOU?*"

D Cartoon published in *Punch*, March 12 1930.

Document questions

1 *Read Document* A. Suggest two reasons why Gandhi wanted the British to get out of India.

2 Compare Documents B and C. What important difference do you notice in these descriptions of what happened? Support your answer with a quotation from each of these two documents.

3 Why do you think Documents B and C are so different? Explain your answer.

4 Compare Gandhi's attitude towards Lord Irwin (Document A) with Lord Irwin's attitude towards the Indians (Document C). Explain one difference and quote from both documents to support your answer.

5 Do you think the person who drew Document D was more likely to have been a supporter or an opponent of Gandhi? Mention clues in the cartoon which help explain your answer.

6 *Look at the documents again and:*
   a explain what you think the words 'civil disobedience' mean, and
   b explain why Gandhi used non-violent civil disobedience rather than any other form of protest.

7 How useful to the historian of Gandhi's salt protest are newspaper reports (as in Document B) as evidence?

Follow-on questions

8 Why do you think the British didn't arrest Gandhi after he had written his letter to Lord Irwin (Document A)? Why do you think they waited until after his salt march?

9 How important do you think Gandhi's non-violent protest tactics were in eventually getting independence for India?

10 As an adviser to Lord Irwin, write a report describing the problems Gandhi's tactics have caused the British government. Suggest ideas for dealing with these problems.

10.2 UDI 1965

A Declaration by Ian Smith, Prime Minister of Rhodesia, November 11 1965.
"We Rhodesians have rejected the doctrinaire philosophy of appeasement and surrender. The decision which we have taken today is a refusal by Rhodesians to sell their birthright. And, even if we were to surrender, does anyone believe that Rhodesia would be the last target of the communists in the Afro-Asian block? We have struck a blow for the preservation of justice, civilization and Christianity: and in the spirit of this belief, we have this day assumed our sovereign independence. God bless you all."

B Article by the Soviet newspaper *Izvestia*, November 11 1965.
"Independence – Racist Style.

Rhodesian UDI is a monstrous crime. Mr Smith's announcement is an impudent challenge to world opinion. Two hundred thousand white colonists have usurped the independent power over the four million population of Zimbabwe."

C Speech by Harold Wilson in the House of Commons, November 11 1965.
"Reason has fled the scene and emotions, unreasoning racialist emotions at that, have taken command, regardless of the conclusions for Rhodesia, Africa and the world. This is an act of rebellion against the crown. It is a tragedy affecting a great people, including many thousands who have made their homes there and of millions more who are denied the human right of self expression and self determination."

D Cartoon in *Private Eye*, November 1965.

Document questions

1 *Read Document* A.
   a Quote two reasons why Ian Smith said he had declared Rhodesia's independence.
   b What do you think the word 'appeasement' means (Document A), and with which period or time in history is this word usually connected?

2 *Read Document* B.
   a By what other name is 'Rhodesia' called?
   b Write a couple of sentences to explain why you think the same country is called by two different names.

3 Explain why the authors of Documents B and C are opposed to Ian Smith. Support your explanation with quotations from the documents.

4 **a** Why do you think Ian Smith chose to use words like 'justice, civilisation, Christianity' in Document A? Explain your answer.
   b Explain why Ian Smith's opponents would object so strongly to his use of the words 'justice, civilisation, Christianity'.

5 *Look at Document* D. Explain the point that the cartoonist was trying to make and support it by mentioning things seen in the cartoon.

Follow-on questions

6 What is a 'unilateral declaration of independence' (a 'UDI')?

7 What clues are there in the documents about the way Ian Smith's government ran Rhodesia before UDI.

8 *Compare these documents with those on 'Apartheid' (page 114).* What similarities in 'white' attitudes do you notice? Support your answer with quotations from the documents.

10.3 Apartheid

A **Speech by Johannes Strydom (later the Prime Minister of South Africa) to the South African Assembly, January 1948, in defence of 'white superiority'.**
"Either you are the boss, or the equal, or the inferior. One of the three. If you are not the boss, you must be a man's equal . . . It is so clear and logical. If you say that you do not want to dominate the native it simply means that you stand for a policy of equality."

B **Map showing approximate distribution of Bantu reserves after the Promotion of Bantu Self Government Act, 1959.**

C **Racial categories as defined by the National Party, 1950.**
"*White:* White person means a person who in appearance obviously is, or who is generally accepted as a white person, but does not include a person who, although in appearance obviously a white person, is generally accepted as a coloured person.
Native: Native means a person who in fact is, or is generally accepted as, a member of any aboriginal race or tribe of Africa.
Coloured person: Coloured person means a person who is not a white person or a native."

D Cartoon from *The Observer*, 1985.

Document questions

1 What evidence is there in Document A to suggest that Johannes Strydom believed that 'whites' were superior to 'natives'?

2 *Look at Document B.*
   a What are 'Bantu reserves'?
   b Opponents of apartheid say it is unfair and immoral. What evidence is there in the map to support this criticism? Explain your answer carefully.

3 *Read Document C.*
   a Write a couple of sentences to explain why you think the National party felt it needed to define who was 'white', 'native' or 'coloured'. You don't need to quote, just write your own words.
   b Opponents of apartheid say that it is a system which cannot work. What evidence is there in Document C to support this criticism? Explain your answer and back it up with a quotation from Document C.

4 *Look at Document D.* What point do you think the cartoonist is making about the system of apartheid? Support your answer by describing and explaining things included in the cartoon.

5 *Look at the documents again.* Suggest two ways in which the ideas about apartheid shown in these documents are similar to the ideas of the Nazis. Support each reason with a quotation from the documents.

Follow-on questions

6 What does the word apartheid mean?

7 Name the South African leader shown on the left hand side of Document D.

8 What similarity do you notice between the ideas expressed in Document A and the words spoken by the man on the left hand side of Document D?

9 If apartheid is such an evil system, how do its supporters justify it? Suggest two reasons they give in justification.

10.4   **Soweto**

A **Tables of statistics about South African education quoted in a UNESCO Report 1976.**

(i) *Primary and secondary education*

	Average amount spent on each pupil		Number of pupils per class		% of pupils entering school in 1963 and reaching	
					8th year	12th year
	1962	1976	1963	1976		
Whites	146	644	23	20	99	58.4
Africans	12	42	58	52	12	0.2

(ii) *Graduates, 1975–1976*

	Whites	Africans
Doctors	601	6
Engineers	1070	2
Biologists	168	0

B **Part of a statement by Dr Hendrik Verwoerd, Minister of Native Affairs, 1954.**
"There is no place for the African in the European Community above the level of certain forms of labour. Within his own community, however, all doors are open.

My department's policy is that Bantu education should stand with both feet in the reserves and with its roots in the spirit and being of Bantu society."

C **Photographs of African education in Soweto.**

D Article by Nat Aiseko, black resident of Soweto and journalist on the *Rand Daily Mail*, June 1976.

"I was born and bred in South Africa. I have no ties with any Bantustan homeland; I was born in an urban area. I find it difficult to understand why a white immigrant does not have to carry a pass all the time while I do; why he is able to buy a house anywhere in the country, rent a house or flat, go to any holiday resort, get a good job, choose where he wants his children to go to school.

I'd like to be able to walk home down a well-lit street to a place I can call home. With television maybe. An electric stove and a bathroom with running hot water would also be great. These might seem little things, but in Soweto and other townships in South Africa, the black man has few of these comforts. Among the million people in Soweto there are a lot of ordinary folk for whom things like money, jobs, clothes, food, family and a sound education are among the most common aspirations.

To these people, thuggery, violence and racial hatred are anathema. But even ordinary people can be pushed to anger and, given the opportunity will vent their frustrations against the objects of oppression."

Document questions

1 *Look at the figures in Document* **A** *(ii).* How do the others figures in Document **A** (i) help explain why there were so few African engineers, yet so many white engineers? In your answer try to write a sentence about each of the three parts of Document **A** (i).

2 *Read Document* **B**. Write a few sentences to explain how the statement in the document helps us understand the figures in the tables. Back up up your answer with a quotation from Document **B**.

3 Describe what you see in Document **C** and write sentences to explain which of the figures in Document **A** they help us understand.

4 **a** Name two ways in which the ideas in Documents **B** and **D** are different.
  b Why do you think the ideas in Documents **B** and **D** are so different?

5 **a** Give reasons suggested in the documents that might help explain why a serious disturbance took place in Soweto in 1976.
  b How useful to the historian of the disturbance in Soweto is the evidence of a Sowetan journalist (document **D**)?

Follow-on questions

6 What is a 'Bantustan homeland' (Document **D**)?

7 How did the career of the author of Document **B** come to an end?

8 What is the name given to the system of separate development which the author of Document **B** helped set up?

10.5 White settlers in Africa

A **Map showing African land conquered by Europeans by 1914.**

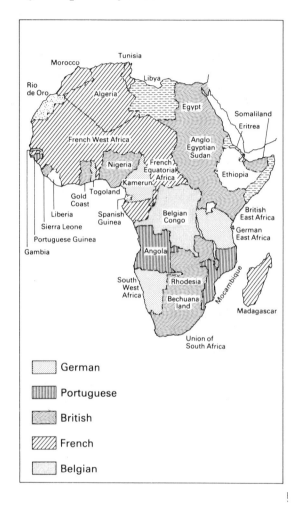

German

Portuguese

British

French

Belgian

B **Description by Chief Kabongo of the Kikuyu tribe of the arrival of a white administrator to his people in the early years of this century.**

"A pink cheek man came one day to our council. He came from far, from where many of their people lived in houses made of stone, and where they had their own council. He sat in our midst and he told us of the king of the pink cheek who was a great king and lived in a land over the seas.

'This great king is now your king', he said 'and this land is all his land, though he has said you may live on it as you are his people and he is your father and you are his sons.' This was strange news, for this land was ours . . . we had no king, we elected our councils and they made our laws . . . With patience, our leading elders tried to tell this to the pink cheek, and he listened. But at the end he said, 'This we know, but in spite of this what I have told you is a fact. You have now a king . . . and in the town called Nairobi is a council or government that acts for the king. And his laws are your laws'."

C **Extract from a statement by Cecil Rhodes, Prime Minister of Cape Colony in the 1890s, written in a letter to W. T. Stead, August 19 1891.**

"I contend that we are the first race in the world and that the more of the world we inhabit the better it is for the human race. I contend that every acre added to our territory provides for the birth of more of the English race, who otherwise would not be brought into existence . . . I believe it to be my duty to God, my Queen and my country to paint the whole map of Africa red, red from the Cape to Cairo. That is my creed, my dream, my mission."

D **From 'Child of Two Worlds' by Mugo Gatheru (a Kenyan who studied in India, USA and Great Britain), 1964.**

"About 17,000 square miles of the best land in Kenya was declared open to white settlers only. The 60,000 Europeans who ruled us could live in these 'white highlands', but the 7,000,000 Africans were made to live largely in 'reserves' – parts of the land set aside just for Africans, like was done to the Indians in North America. This created strong and deep feelings among my people that they had not been treated right. How can there be an exclusive 'white highlands' in the black man's country?"

Document questions

1 *Look at Document* [A]. Name the only two African countries not under European control by 1914.

2 *Read Document* [B].
   a What evidence is there to suggest that the Europeans might think the Africans were uncivilised?
   b What evidence is there to suggest that the Africans might think that the Europeans were uncivilised?
   c How fair is it to conclude from the evidence in Document [B] that the Africans knew nothing about democracy? Explain your answer and support it with a quotation from Document [B].

3 *Read Document* [C] *and look at Document* [A]. What was Rhodes' dream and how far had it come true by 1914?

4 *Read Documents* [C] *and* [D]. How do the attitudes held by Britons like Rhodes (Document [C]) help explain why the British felt they could take the best land in Kenya (Document [D])? Explain your answer and support it with a quotation from Document [C].

5 What clues are there in the documents to help explain why European rule in Africa eventually came to an end? Support your answer with quotations.

Follow-on questions

6 Why do Rhodes' attitudes (Document [C]) seem so strange today?

7 *Read Document* [D]. Suggest two similarities between European rule in Kenya and the apartheid system in South Africa.

11.1   The space race

A **Statement by American astronaut Neil Armstrong, as he became the first man to walk on the moon, July 21 1969.**
"One small step for man, one giant leap for mankind."

B **From 'Space History' by Tony Osman, 1983.**
"It would be easy, though not completely accurate, to say that the Americans invaded the moon because they had failed in a military invasion. In 1961 President Kennedy was persuaded by his Central Intelligence Agency that the Cubans were ready to rebel against their President, Fidel Castro, and that a landing would be welcomed and successful. None of these statements was true and the Americans were soundly defeated in the Bay of Pigs in April 1961. This was just three months after he was sworn in as President. Kennedy needed a popular crusade that would restore America's belief in itself, in its image in the eyes of the world and, far from incidentally, in his own ability.

The project attracted Kennedy: a moon-landing would be a splendid realisation of the phrase which had characterised his election campaign, 'the new frontier'. And NASA's advice seemed more reliable than that of the CIA. In his address to Congress on 25 May 1961, Kennedy made his historic declaration: 'I believe that this nation should commit itself to achieving the goal, before the decade is out, of landing a man on the moon and returning him safely to earth'. He backed his statement with a large increase in NASA's funds, and the project was named Apollo."

C **Interview given on American TV, July 21 1969, by Lyndon B. Johnson, former President of the United States (1963–1968).**
"The challenge of space is beneficial. As I see it, if space can be conquered, so too can domestic problems. Aid for education and medical care for the aged would be among the direct results of the space program . . . Space achievements have increased America's stature in the world, and to prove this I have a letter of thanks from Ho Chi Minh for a photograph of the world taken from Apollo 8."

D **'US doubts on eve of moon adventure', newspaper article in the *Times* by its correspondent in Washington, Ian Macdonald, July 10 1969.**
"To a quite surprising degree the Americans that any foreigner in this country meets on a day to day basis – Washington or New York thinkers, officials and professionals – reveal strangely embarrassed feelings on the eve of man's first landing on the moon.

It is true that there must be millions across the nation who believe in the values and scales of national achievement. They will sit up all night before their televisions to watch Mr Neil Armstrong step out in the early hours of July 21.

When an inquiring reporter notes that more columns and popular attention is being given to Apollo 11 in Britain and Europe, the frequent reply is a shrug of the shoulders and the comment: 'You people don't have to pay for it'. Observers contrast the relative ease with which the Apollo programme managers have been able to obtain the needed funds with the struggle of the poverty programme to stay alive and the pressing need of the cities for housing and services."

E **Cartoon from *Punch*, 1969.**

"Don't you feel comforted at the thought of all the benefits it'll bring to future generations?"

Document questions

1 *Read Document* A. Explain carefully what you think Neil Armstrong meant when he described the landing on the moon as a 'giant leap for mankind'.

2 *Read Documents* B *and* C.
   a Which one is the primary source and which is the secondary source? Explain your answer.
   b In what way might the primary source be biased?

3 Name one primary source of evidence that the author of Document B quotes, and explain why it could be useful to a historian of space exploration.

4 *Read Documents* C *and* D. If landing on the moon was such a great achievement, why did some Americans seem to have doubts about it? Explain your answer and support it with a quotation from one of the documents.

5 **a** What point do you think the person who drew Document E was trying to make? Support your answer by mentioning things seen in the cartoon.
   b Do you think the person who drew Document E would have agreed more with Document B or with Document C as to the real reasons behind the space programme? Give reasons for your answer.

Follow-on questions

6 Who was Ho Chi Minh (Document C) and why is it surprising that he should send President Johnson a letter of thanks?

7 How did L. B. Johnson become President of the USA?

8 What steps had the USSR taken before 1961 to put itself in the lead in the space race?

11.2 The hydrogen bomb

A **The USA begins production of the hydrogen bomb – statement by President Truman, January 31 1949.**
"It is part of my responsibility as commander-in chief of the armed forces to see to it that our country is able to defend itself against any possible aggressor. Accordingly I have ordered the Atomic Energy Commission to continue its work on all forms of atomic energy weapons, including the so-called hydrogen or super-bomb. Like all other work in the field of atomic weapons, it is being and will be part of our program for peace and security. This we shall continue to do until a satisfactory plan for control of atomic energy is achieved."

B **The USSR announces that it has the hydrogen bomb – speech by Soviet Prime Minister Malenkov to the Supreme Soviet of the USSR on August 8 1953.**
"The warmongers abroad convinced themselves that the USA had a monopoly of the atomic bomb. History, however, showed this to be very wrong. The United States no longer has a monopoly in the production of atomic bombs. The transatlantic enemies of peace have of late found a new weapon. They say that the United States . . . is in possession of a still more powerful weapon than the atom bomb, and has the monopoly of the hydrogen bomb. This could have been some sort of comfort for them had it been true. But this is not so. The government feels that it is necessary to report to the Supreme Soviet that the United States has no monopoly in the production of the hydrogen bomb either."

C **The USSR announces that it has exploded a hydrogen bomb, 1972.**
"It was announced in *Pravda* on August 20 that the Soviet Union had exploded a hydrogen bomb, this being the first claim by any country to have detonated this weapon. The announcement, which was not given special prominence and appeared on an inner page, stated that the explosion was 'of great strength' and had shown that the power of the hydrogen bomb was 'many times greater than the power of atomic bombs'. The paper gave an assurance on behalf of the Soviet government that there was 'no foundation for alarm', emphasizing in this connection that the Soviet Union continued to stand for the all-round reduction of armaments, a ban on all weapons of mass destruction and the enforcement of 'strict international control of this ban by the United Nations'."

D **British cartoon, January 20 1950.**

MARCH OF SCIENCE

Document questions

1 According to Document [A], why was the USA beginning production of the hydrogen bomb?

2 According to Document [B], why did the USSR find it necessary to have the hydrogen bomb?

3 What was so special about the hydrogen bomb compared to earlier bombs?

4 *Compare Documents* [A] *and* [C]. What similarity do you notice between American and Soviet reasons for having the hydrogen bomb?

5 *Look at Document* [D].
  a Why is 'Civilisation' looking so worried?
  b Why do you think the cartoon is called the 'March of Science'? What point do you think the cartoonist is trying to make?

6 Document [A] states that the development of the hydrogen bomb is 'part of the program for peace and security'. Do you think the cartoonist would agree with this view about the hydrogen bomb? Give reasons for your answer.

7 Document [C] states that the Soviet Union 'continued to stand for the all-round reduction of armaments, a ban of all weapons of mass destruction'. What other evidence is there in Document [C] which does not seem to agree with this statement?

Follow-on questions

8 What part did President Truman play in the nuclear arms race (Document [A])?

9 Compare cartoon [D] with the cartoon on page 14. They were both drawn by the same person. What similarity do you notice in the points he is trying to make in these cartoons?

11.3   East–West disarmament

One problem that both sides have found in disarmament talks is that it's difficult to agree how many weapons each side has – and how to compare those weapons. You can find out more about these problems by studying these sets of figures.

A NATO and the Warsaw Pact – the facts.

(i) *Ground forces in Europe*

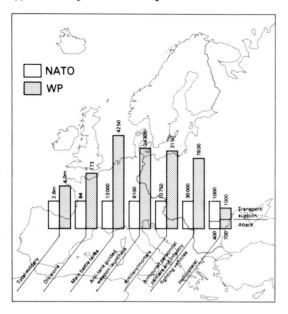

(ii) *Air forces in Europe*

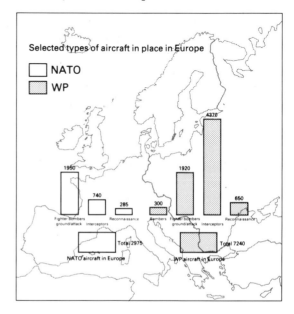

B The East–West conventional balance in 1982.

(i)

Ground forces: Europe only	NATO	Warsaw Pact
Total ground forces	2.1 millions	1.7 millions
Main battle tanks	17,100	26,300
Artillery tubes	9,500	10,000
Anti-tank guided weapon launchers	5,800	1,400
Surface-to-air missile launchers	1,800	3,200

(ii)

Air forces: Europe only	NATO	Warsaw Pact
Bombers	80	370
Attack/fighter aircraft	2,500	2,420
Air defence aircraft	570	1,490
Helicopters	730	160

Document questions

1 According to Document A (i), which side, NATO or the Warsaw Pact, appears to have the stronger ground forces in Europe? Quote figures from the chart to support your explanation.

2 *Look at Document A (ii) (air forces in Europe).* Explain whether you think this gives a broadly similar, or very different view of the military balance between the two sides, from that given in Document A (i). Quote figures from Document A (ii) to support your answer.

3 *Compare Documents B (i) and A (i)*
  a Describe two important differences in the way these two charts show the balance between the two sides. Quote figures from Document B (i) to support each of the answers.
  b Look at the things being compared in Documents B (i) and A (i). Explain why it might be misleading, or unfair, to compare figures in these two charts.

4 *Compare Documents B (ii) and A (ii).*
  a What important difference do you notice in the total number of aircraft shown for each of the two sides in these two charts?
  b Suggest a reason for this difference. Explain your answer.

5 Why do you think Documents A (i) and A (ii) were produced? What do they show and what message do they put across?

6 How do these documents help explain why it is difficult to make disarmament talks succeed?

7 What problems might the historian of disarmament talks have in using statistics like those shown in these documents as evidence?

Follow-on questions

8 **a** What is
    i. NATO,
    ii. the Warsaw Pact?
  b When and why were they set up?

Acknowledgements

The author would like to express his grateful thanks to Jane Bishop for typing the manuscript and to Jill Kates for help with the research.

The author and publishers are very grateful to the following for permission to reproduce documents. While every effort has been made to trace copyright holders this has not been possible in every case. The Publishers apologise for any omissions and, if notified, will correct the matter at the next printing.

Of particular value to students of twentieth century history is the journal Keesings Contemporary Archives (retitled as Keesings' Record of World Events with effect from January 1987, and published by Longman Group UK). Some of the many extracts from Keesings used in this book, for which the author and publishers are most grateful, have been abridged or edited.

The Imperial War Museum (cat. no. MH 13418): imprint page; A The Daily Mirror: page 8; B Translation by John Hamer, first appeared in *The Twentieth Century* published by Macmillan, London and Basingstoke: page 8; C source unknown: page 10; D Longman: page 9; E Popperfoto: page 10; F University of London, Weiner Library: page 11; G Bilderdienst Süddeutscher Verlag: page 12; H University of London, Weiner Library: page 12; I University of London, Weiner Library: page 13; J The Imperial War Museum (cat. no. MW 6790): page 14; K First published in *The Evening Standard*: page 14; 1.1 The Mary Evans Picture Library; 1.1 A The Trustees of the Imperial War Museum, London (cat. no. POS 77); 1.1 B Collins, 1972 and reproduced by permission of INPRA; 1.1 C Croom Helm; 1.2 C The Mary Evans Picture Library; 1.2 D Reproduced in *Eye-Deep in Hell* by John Ellis, Croom Helm, 1979; 1.2 E The Trustees of the Imperial War Museum, London (cat. no. Q 111501); 1.3 A The Fawcett Library/Mary Evans Picture Library; 1.3 B The Trustees of the Imperial War Museum, London (cat. no. Q 33085); 1.3 C Macdonald (Publishers); 1.3 D From information quoted in *Suffragettes International* by Trevor Lloyd, Macdonald, 1971; 1.4 A/D The Trustees of the Imperial War Museum, London (cat. nos. Q 825–38, Q 81147, Q 46428 and Q 48378A); 1.5 Sir David Low from *The Evening Standard*; 1.5 D Originally published by Hutchinson; 2.1 A Basil Blackwell; 2.1 B Bernard Partridge/Punch Publications; 2.1 C/D Taken from *Britain, Europe and the Modern World* by Paul Richardson, Heinemann Educational Books; 2.1 E Original publisher not known but reproduced in *A Coursebook of Modern World History* by P. F. Speed, Arnold Wheaton; 2.2 A/B The Photo Source; 2.2 C SCM Press Ltd.; 2.2 D Quoted in *The World Book Encyclopaedia*, 1979, World-book–Childcraft International Inc.; 2.3 A From United States Department of State Bulletin; 2.3 B Sir David Low from *The Evening Standard*; 2.3 C United Nations General Assembly Official Records; 2.3 D The School of Slavonic and East European Studies, University of London; 2.4 A United States Government Printing Office, Washington D.C.; 2.4 B United States Library of Congress; 2.4 C United Nations General Assembly Official Records; 2.4 D The School of Slavonic and East European Studies, University of London; 2.5 A The Novosti Press, Moscow; 2.5 B The School of Slavonic and East European Studies, University of London; 2.5 C Keesings Contemporary Archives 1950; 2.5 D Sir David Low from *The Evening Standard*; 2.6 B *The Guardian*; 2.6 C The Associated Press; 2.7 A From *Stalin: A Political Biography* by Isaac Deutscher, Oxford University Press, 1949; 2.7 B The Elsie Timbey Collection, Society for Cultural Relations with the USSR; 2.7 C W. H. Allen and reproduced by permission of the author; 2.7 D From *Joseph Stalin: Man and Legend* by Ronald Hingley, Hutchinson and reproduced by permission of the author; 2.8 A The Trustees of the British Museum; 2.8 B From *Joseph Stalin: Man and Legend* by Ronald Hingley, Hutchinson and reproduced by permission of the author; 2.8 C Oxford University Press; 2.8 D Quoted in *The World since 1900* by Tony Howarth Longman 1979; 2.9 A Oxford University Press; 2.9 B Hutchinson and reproduced by permission of the author; 2.9 C The School of Slavonic and East European Studies, University of London; 2.10 A The British Atlantic Committee; 2.10 B The Novosti Press, Moscow; 2.10 C/D The School of Slavonic and East European Studies, University of London; 2.11 A/B Keesings Contemporary Archives 1968; 2.11 C J. K./Magnum, John Hillelson Ltd.; 2.12 A/B Keesings Contemporary Archives 1980; 2.12 C Gerald Scarfe; 2.12 D Keesings Contemporary Archives 1980; 3.1 A/B The School of Slavonic and East European Studies, University of London; 3.1 C United States Department of State Bulletin; 3.1 D From V. M. Molotov's *Problems of Foreign Policy: Speeches and Statements, April 1946–November 1948* published in Moscow, 1949 (publisher unknown); 3.2 A From *The Post War Speeches of Winston Churchill*, Cassell and reproduced by permission of Macmillan and Co. Inc.; 3.2 B Leslie Illingworth from *The Daily Mail*; 3.2 C First appeared in Soviet newspaper *Pravda*; 3.2 D The School of Slavonic and East European Studies, University of London; 3.3 A/B Keesings Contemporary Archives 1960; 3.3 C 'Vicky' from *The New Statesman*; 3.4 B Longman; 3.4 C Keesings Contemporary Archives 1960; 4.1 C The Trustees of the Imperial War Museum, London (cat. no. NYP 68056); 4.1 D Ballantine/Random House Inc. and reproduced by permission of Doubleday & Co. Inc.; 4.2 A Weidenfeld (Publishers) Limited; 4.2 B Sidney Strube from *The Daily Express*; 4.2 C Part of the Wayland Documentary series; 4.2 D Sir David Low from *The Evening Standard*; 4.3 B Weidenfeld (Publishers) Limited; 4.3 C/D The Institute of Contemporary History and Wiener Library; 4.4 B Weidenfeld (Publishers) Limited; 4.4 C Oxford University Press, 1949; 4.4 D The Institute of Contemporary History and Wiener Library; 4.4 E The Associated Press; 4.4 F The Elsie Timbey Collection, Society for Cultural Relations with the USSR; 5.1 A Cassell and reproduced by permission of Times Books Ltd.; 5.1 B Ernest Shepard/Punch Publications Ltd.;

5.1 C Pelican, and reproduced by permission of Penguin Books Ltd.; 5.1 D Weidenfeld (Publishers) Limited; 5.2 A Ballantine/Random House Inc. and reproduced by permission of Doubleday Inc.; 5.2 B Collins Publishers; 5.2 C Ernest Shepard/Punch Publications; 5.3 A Leslie Illingworth/Punch Publications; 5.3 C Sidgwick & Jackson; 5.3 D/5.4 A Sir David Low from *The Evening Standard*; 5.4 B W. H. Allen and reproduced by permission of the author; 5.4 C From *The Twentieth Century*, edited by A. J. P. Taylor, published by N.C.L.S.; 6.1 A Orbis Publishers Ltd.; 6.1 B Book Club Associates; 6.1 C Sidney Strube from *The Daily Express*; 6.1 D From *The First Casualty* by P. Knightly, Quartet Books; 6.2 B Quoted in *The War Papers*, Way and Cavendish; 6.2 C BBC Hulton Picture Library; 6.2 D Quartet Books; 6.3 A/E The Trustees of the Imperial War Museum, London (cat. nos. MW 7406, MW 13644, MW 13594, MH 13802 and MW 13585); 6.4 A/B The Museums Department, City of Portsmouth; 6.4 C The Trustees of the Imperial War Museum, London (cat. no. B 5245); 6.4 D The Museums Department, City of Portsmouth; 6.5 B Copyright holder unknown but held in the Institute of Contemporary History and Wiener Library; 6.5 C Auschwitz State Museum, Poland; 6.5 D From *Auschwitz* an exhibition publication from the East London Auschwitz Committee; 6.5 E The Photo Source; 6.6 A Original publisher unknown but reproduced in *A Coursebook of Modern World History* by P. F. Speed, Arnold Wheaton; 6.6 B The Novosti Press, Moscow; 6.6 C The Campaign for Nuclear Disarmament; 6.6 D 'Vicky' from *The Evening Standard*; 7.1 A/B Quoted in *Red Star over China* by Edgar Snow, published by Victor Gollancz; 7.1 C Orbis Publishing Limited; 7.1 D Franklin Watts Inc.; 7.2 A Marc Riboud/Magnum, John Hillelson Ltd. 7.2 B Quoted in *The Political Thoughts of Mao Tse Tung*, Stuart Schram; 7.2 C The Bodley Head; 7.2 D The Novosti Press, Moscow; 7.3 A The Anglo-Chinese Educational Institute; 7.3 C Georg Gerster/John Hillelson Ltd.; 7.4 A Sygmachine/John Hillelson Ltd.; 7.4 B Quoted in *A Revolution is not a Dinner Party* by Richard Solomon, Anchor Press/Doubleday; 8.1 A/E Keesings Contemporary Archives 1956; 8.2 C/D Keesings Contemporary Archives 1967; 8.3 A/B Keesings Contemporary Archives 1970; 8.3 C United Nations General Assembly Official Records; 8.3 D Quoted in *On the Warpath* by John Cox, published by Oxford University Press; 8.3 E Popperfoto; 8.3 F Keesings Contemporary Archives 1970; 8.4 A/D Keesings Contemporary Archives 1979; 9.1 A/C Keesings Contemporary Archives 1950; 9.1 D Sir David Low from *The Evening Standard*; 9.2 A Bruce Davidson/Magnum, John Hillelson Ltd.; 9.2 B Programme directed by Sharon Sopher; Developing News Inc.; 9.2 C Keesings Contemporary Archives 1954; 9.2 D Quoted in *Black in a White World*, Economist Brief 5, published by The Economist Newspapers Ltd., 1967; 9.3 A Quoted in *Mahatma Gandhi* by B. R. Nanada, George Allen & Unwin, 1978 and reproduced by permission of the author; 9.3 B From *What Manner of Man* by Lerone Bennett, George Allen & Unwin, 1966; 9.3 C Bob Henriques/Magnum, John Hillelson Ltd.; 9.3 D Leonard Freed/Magnum, John Hillelson Ltd.; 9.4 A Quoted in *The U.K. Press Gazette*, Dec. 1970; 9.4 C Published in *Dateline*, the New York Overseas Press Club publication; 9.4 D Quoted in an article by Marina Warner, from *The Spectator*, July 1972; 9.4 E The Associated Press; 10.1 A Quoted in *Mahatma Ghandi* by B. R. Nanada, published by George Allen & Unwin, 1978 and reproduced by permission of the author; 10.1 B Quoted in *Mahatma Gandhi and his Apostles* by Ved Mehta, André Deutsch; 10.1 C Quoted in *The Essential Gandhi* by Lovis Firscher, George Allen & Unwin, 1963; 10.1 D Ravenhill/Punch Publications; 10.2 A/C Keesings Contemporary Archives 1965; 10.2 D Gerald Scarfe; 10.3 A Quoted in *The White Tribe of Africa* by David Harrison, BBC Publications, 1981; 10.3 C Taken from the National Party Election Manifesto 1984; 10.3 D KAL/Kevin Kallaugher; 10.4 B Keesings Contemporary Archives 1954; 10.4 C The International Defence and Aid Fund for Southern Africa; 10.5 A/B From *A Plague of Europeans* by D. Killingray, Penguin Educational/Penguin Books Ltd.; 10.5 C From *Review of Reviews 1902*; 10.5 D Heinemann; 10.1 B Michael Joseph; 11.1 C/D *The Times*; 11.1 E Roy Raymonde/Punch Publications; 11.2 A Keesings Contemporary Archives 1949; 11.2 B Keesings Contemporary Archives 1953; 11.2 C Keesings Contemporary Archives 1972; 11.2 D Sir David Low from *The Evening Standard*; 11.3 A Based on material from the British Atlantic Education Committee, 1984; 11.3 B Based on material from *The Roots of European Security*, Novosti Press, Moscow.

Index